OCS Study
MMS 2004-022

Subsurface, High-Speed Current Jets in the Deepwater Region of the Gulf of Mexico

I0439086

Final Report

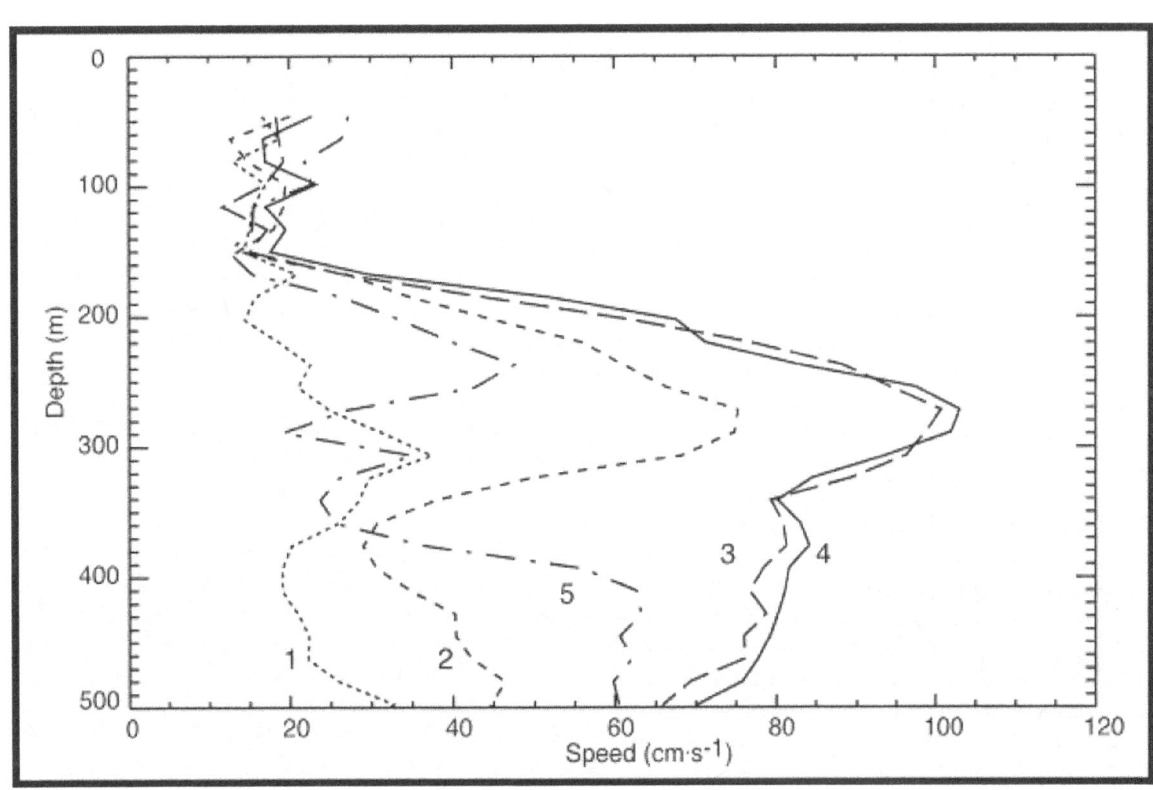

U.S. Department of the Interior
Minerals Management Service
Gulf of Mexico OCS Region

OCS Study
MMS 2004-022

Subsurface, High-Speed Current Jets in the Deepwater Region of the Gulf of Mexico

Final Report

Authors

Steven F. DiMarco
Matthew K. Howard
Worth D. Nowlin, Jr.
Robert O. Reid

Prepared under MMS Contract
1435-01-99-CT-31026
by
Texas A&M University
Department of Oceanography
College Station, Texas

Published by

U.S. Department of the Interior
Minerals Management Service
Gulf of Mexico OCS Region

New Orleans
July 2004

DISCLAIMER

This report was prepared under contract between the Minerals Management Service and the Texas A&M Research Foundation. This report has been technically reviewed by the MMS and approved for publication. Approval does not signify that the contents necessarily reflect the views and policies of the Service, nor does mention of trade names or commercial products constitute endorsement or recommendation for use. It is, however, exempt from review and compliance with MMS editorial standards.

REPORT AVAILABILITY

Extra copies of the report may be obtained from the Public Information Office (Mail Stop 5034) at the following address:

U.S. Department of the Interior
Minerals Management Service
Gulf of Mexico OCS Region
Public Information Office (MS 5034)
1201 Elmwood Park Boulevard
New Orleans, Louisiana 70123-2394

Telephone: (504) 736 2519 or
1-800-200-GULF

CITATION

Suggested citation:

DiMarco, S.F., M.K. Howard, W.D. Nowlin Jr., and R.O. Reid. 2004. Subsurface, high-speed current jets in the deepwater region of the Gulf of Mexico. U.S. Dept. of the Interior, Minerals Management Service, Gulf of Mexico OCS Region, New Orleans, LA. OCS Study MMS 2004-022. 98 pp.

ABOUT THE COVER

The cover art shows vertical profiles of current speed versus depth from a 75-kHz acoustic Doppler current profiler during an 8-hour period from 2135 UTC 10 February 1997 to 0535 UTC 11 February 1997. Profiles are two hours apart; measurement location is lease block VK956 (29.045°N, 88.094°W). The record shows the development of a subsurface, high-speed current jet which exceeded 100 cm·s^{-1} at 275 m below the sea surface. Data are courtesy of Shell Oil Company.

ACKNOWLEDGMENTS

This report would not have been possible without the contributions of many people who contributed observational data, numerical output from ocean circulation models, and experiences and perspectives from the offshore drilling industry. The principal investigators and their tasks for the Jets Project are:

Worth D. Nowlin, Jr.	Program Manager, Principal Investigator
Steven F. DiMarco	Deputy Program Manager, Task Leader: Data Analysis and Physical mechanisms
Matthew K. Howard	Task Leader: data and model output inventory
Robert O. Reid	Co-Leader: Physical mechanisms

A number of individuals from several oil companies were instrumental for providing access and permission to display proprietary data sets, instrument deployment documentation, and industry reports. Special thanks go to: David Driver (BP/AMOCO), Cort Cooper (Chevron/Texaco), Thomas Mitchell (Texaco), Ken Schaudt (Marathon Oil Co.), Michael Vogel and George Forristall (Shell Oil Co.), Dave Peters (Conoco), and Dave Szabo (FugroGEOS).

Numerical model outputs were provided for analysis by: Lakshmi Kantha and J. K. Choi (CU), Lewis Rothstein, Sergei Frolov, and Dail Rowe (AEF), William Jobst and Tamara Townsend (NRL), Leo Oey (Princeton), and Steve Morey (FSU).

We thank the members of the three other MMS Gulf of Mexico Numerical Modeling Studies for useful and stimulating discussion and feedback during annual review meetings: Lewis Rothstein, Sergei Frolov, and Dail Rowe (AEF), Tony Sturges (FSU), Peter Hamilton and Van Waddell (SAIC), Leo Oey (Princeton). In addition, the MMS Model Review Group also provided very useful advice, direction, and criticism throughout the study: Dong-Ping Wang (SUNY), John Allen (OSU), Walter Johnson and Ron Lai (MMS). AEF and Leo Oey also provided specialized contributions for specific inclusion in this report.

We thank Ou Wang for technical assistance and Ann Jochens (TAMU) for useful discussions and insight and for providing specialized plots of altimeter data. We thank Robert Leben (University of Colorado) for providing altimeter data and use of his interactive webpage to produce sea surface height plots. We thank the Ocean Remote Sensing Group of the Johns Hopkins University Applied Physics Laboratory for access to their archive of historical sea surface temperature of the Gulf of Mexico.

Finally, we thank the MMS Contracting Officer's Technical Representatives (COTR) Drs. Alexis Lugo-Fernandez and Carole Current. Their enthusiasm and guidance throughout the Study contributed greatly to its success, particularly since this work challenged many basic assumptions of current measurement and general circulation models.

The Jets Principal Investigators

TABLE OF CONTENTS

PAGE

List of Figures... ix

List of Tables xiii

Acronyms and Abbreviations xv

1. Executive Summary 1

2. Introduction.. 3

    2.1 Background and Program Objectives 3

    2.2 Definition of Subsurface Jet 5

    2.3 Importance to MMS and Offshore Industry 5

    2.4 Data and Output Descriptions 6

    2.5 Report Organization 8

3. Observations 11

    3.1 Descriptions of Jet Candidates 11

        3.1.1 Jet 1 in MC72: 19 April 1990 13

        3.1.2 Jet 2 in GC200: 30 April 1994 15

        3.1.3 Jet 3 in AT575: 16 July 1995 18

        3.1.4 Jet 5 in VK956: 10 February 1997 18

        3.1.5 Jet 6 in MC628: 10 April 1997 25

        3.1.6 Jet 7 in GC505: 4 November 1997 25

        3.1.7 Jet 8 in GC505: 20 November 1997 34

        3.1.8 Jet 9 in GC236: 9 April 1998 34

        3.1.9 Jet 10 in DC977: 28 September 1998 34

        3.1.10 Jet 11 in GC506: 25 October 1998 40

        3.1.11 Jet 12 in EW913: 16 August 1999.. 40

    3.2 ADCP Instrumentation Issues 47

        3.2.1 Structural Interference 47

        3.2.2 Homogeneous Flow Assumption 52

4. Model Studies 59

    4.1 CUPOM Analysis 59

    4.2 PROFS CGS and FGS Analysis 67

    4.3 NLOM Analysis.. 74

    4.4 AEF Analysis.. 78

        4.4.1 Topographic Interaction... 78

        4.4.2 Baroclinic Instability 78

5. Mechanisms 83

    5.1 Summary of Plausible Physical Mechanisms... 83

        5.1.1 Baroclinic Instability 83

        5.1.2 Inertial Wave Train.. 86

        5.1.3 Reversed Baroclinicity 87

        5.1.4 Filament of Loop Current or Loop Current Eddy 87

    5.2 Summary of Possible (But Unlikely) Physical Mechanisms................... 87

        5.2.1 Internal Solitary Waves 87

        5.2.2 Flow Over Undulating Bottom... 90

TABLE OF CONTENTS (continued)

	PAGE
5.3 Additional Annotated References Possibly Relevant to Submerged Jets	90
6. Measurement Recommendations	93
6.1 General Recommendations for Measurements on Offshore Platforms	93
6.2 Specific Recommendations for Jets	94
7. References	97

LIST OF FIGURES

FIGURE		PAGE
2.4-1.	PROFS model probe locations in the Gulf of Mexico.	9
2.4-2.	The Gulf of Mexico subdomains of Leo Oey's PROFS FGS model.	10
3.1-1.	Locations of candidate occurrences of mid-depth current jets in the Gulf of Mexico from public and restricted current observational data sets.	12
3.1.1-1.	Profiles of current speed and direction from lowered S4 current meter at lease block MC72 during jet event on 19 April 1990.	14
3.1.2-1.	Top: Contours of current speed versus depth and time showing subsurface jet occurring in lease block GC200 during 29 April 1994. Bottom: Contours of percentage of good pings per sampling ensemble versus depth and time at same time and location as top panel.	16
3.1.2-2.	Sea-surface height field from satellite altimeter data for 30 April 1994 for GC200 case.	17
3.1.3-1.	Contours of current speed versus depth and time showing subsurface jet occurring in lease block AT575.	19
3.1.3-2.	Sea-surface height field from satellite altimeter data for 6 July 1995 for AT575 case.	20
3.1.3-3.	Contours of percentage of good pings per sampling ensemble versus depth and time at same location as Figure 3.1.3-1.	21
3.1.4-1.	Current profiles made from ADCP two hours apart during the period 2135 UTC 10 February 1997 to 0535 UTC 11 February 1997.	22
3.1.4-2.	Profiles of vertical velocity made two hours apart during 2135 UTC 10 February 1997 to 0535 UTC 11 February 1997.	23
3.1.4-3.	Sea-surface height field from satellite altimeter data for 10 Feb 1997 for VK956 case.	24
3.1.5-1.	Contours of current speed versus depth and time showing subsurface jet occurring in lease block MC628.	26
3.1.5-2.	Contours of percentage of good pings per sampling ensemble versus depth and time at same time and location as Figure 3.1.5-1.	27
3.1.5-3.	Contours of vertical velocity versus depth and time at same time and location as Figure 3.1.5-1.	28
3.1.5-4.	Sea-surface height field from satellite altimeter data for 10 April 1997 for MC628 Jet.	29
3.1.5-5.	AVHRR image of sea-surface temperature of the Gulf of Mexico on 10 Apr 1997.	30
3.1.6-1.	Contours of current speed versus depth and time showing subsurface jet occurring in lease block GC505 during 4 November 1997.	31
3.1.6-2.	Sea-surface height field from satellite altimeter data for 9 November 1997 for GC505 long case.	32
3.1.6-3.	Contours of percentage of good pings per sampling ensemble versus depth and time at the same time and location as Figure 3.1.6-1.	33

LIST OF FIGURES (continued)

FIGURE   PAGE

3.1.7-1.   Contours of current speed versus depth and time showing subsurface
            jet oscillations occurring in lease block GC505 on 20 November 1997.......   35

3.1.7-2.   Contours of percentage of good pings per sampling interval versus
            depth and time at same location as Figure 3.1.7-1.   36

3.1.8-1.   Top: Contours of current speed versus depth and time showing
            subsurface jet occurring in lease block GC236. Bottom: Contours of
            vertical velocity versus depth and time.   37

3.1.8-2.   Sea-surface height of the Gulf of Mexico based on blended
            TOPEX/Poseidon and ERS-2 satellite altimeter on 12 April 1998
            during GC236 jet event.   38

3.1.8-3.   AVHRR image of sea surface temperature of the Gulf of Mexico on
            12 April 1998 during GC236 jet event.   39

3.1.9-1.   Current components from 18-29 hr band-passed records from mooring
            C3 in MMS-sponsored DeSoto Canyon Eddy Intrusion Study located
            in 1,300-m water depth.   41

3.1.9-2.   Sea-surface height field from satellite altimeter data for 28 Sept 1998
            for DC977 case.   42

3.1.9-3.   AVHRR image of sea-surface temperature of the Gulf of Mexico on
            28 September 1998.   43

3.1.10-1.   Sea-surface height field from satellite altimeter data for 25 October
            1998 for GC506 case.   44

3.1.10-2.   Contours of current speed versus depth and time showing subsurface
            jet occurring in lease block GC506.   45

3.1.10-3.   Contours of percentage of good pings per sampling interval versus
            depth and time at same location as Figure 3.1.10-2.   46

3.1.11-1.   Screen image of ADCP control screen on 0614 UTC 16 Aug 1999 for
            EW913 case showing profile of speed and direction versus depth.   48

3.1.11-2.   Screen image of ADCP control screen on 0614 UTC 16 Aug 1999 for
            EW913 case showing profiles of vertical and error velocities versus
            depth.   49

3.1.11-3.   Sea-surface height field from satellite altimeter data for 16 Aug 1999
            for EW913 case.   50

3.1.11-4.   AVHRR image of sea-surface temperature of the Gulf of Mexico on
            16 Aug 1999.   51

3.2.2-1.   Schematic of projection of two-dimensional velocity vector onto
            acoustic radial lines.   53

3.2.2-2.   Schematic of projections of two-dimensional current velocity for
            nonhomogeous case.   55

4.1-1.   Map of north-central Gulf of Mexico south of Mississippi River delta
            showing locations of observed high-speed subsurface jets and virtual
            current meter arrays based on model outputs of PROFS model and
            CUPOM.   61

4.1-2.   Contours of speed versus depth and time during subsurface event M2
            seen in the CUPOM output at five locations along 90°W.   62

x

LIST OF FIGURES (continued)

FIGURE   PAGE

4.1-3.   Sea-surface height field from satellite altimeter data for 17 May 1993 for M2 case. 64

4.1-4.   Three-dimensional view of M2 jet showing sea-surface height, the 50 cm·s⁻¹ isosurface, and horizontal velocity. 65

4.1-5.   Contours of speed versus depth and time during subsurface event M1 seen in the CUPOM output at five locations along 88°W. 66

4.1-6.   Contours of speed versus depth and time during subsurface event M3 seen in the CUPOM output at five locations along 88°W. 68

4.1-7.   Locations of model stations where model speeds anywhere between 200 and 500 m exceeded both 45 cm·s⁻¹ and the vertically-averaged speed for levels in the depth range 50-100 m. 69

4.2-1.   Current speed from PROFS model output at site near lease block AT575: a) no data assimilation, b) with data assimilation. 70

4.2-2.   Left: 18-29 hr band-pass filtered current velocity at 12, 72, and 500 m depths at the MMS Eddy Intrusion Study mooring C3 during Hurricane Georges. Right: Raw current component velocities taken from PROFS FGS model run at depths 10, 70, and 500 m. 72

4.2-3.   Top: Depth of isotherm versus time from FGS version of PROFS model from model year 1 Jan 1998 through 30 June 1998. Middle: Contours of speed versus depth and time. Bottom: Difference of speed maximum between 150 and 300 m and surface speed versus depth and time. 73

4.2-4.   Contours and vectors of current speed from FGS PROFS model on 11 April 1998. 75

4.3-1.   Sea-surface height field of north-central Gulf of Mexico from 1/16° Global NLOM model on 1 August 1999. 76

4.3-2.   Current vectors and speed contours from 1/16° Global NLOM on 16 August 1999 from three model layer depths: 80, 400, and 600 m. 77

4.4.1-1.   Simulation of a cyclone being squeezed between an LCE and topography. 79

4.4.2-1.   Unstable surface-intensified frontal structure and potential vorticity and velocity fields in the midwater column after 30 days of model integration. 81

4.4.2-2.   Unstable mid-depth-intensified frontal structure and potential vorticity and velocity fields in the midcolumn after 60 days of integration. 82

5.1.1-1.   Sea-surface height of the Gulf of Mexico from satellite altimeter data for 26 April 2001. 85

5.1.1-2.   AVHRR image of sea-surface temperature of the Gulf of Mexico on 26 April 2001. 86

5.1.3-1.   Radial sections through (a) an anticyclone and (b) a cyclone. 88

5.2.1-1.   Internal soliton in a two-layer fluid of finite depth. 89

LIST OF TABLES

TABLE		PAGE
3.1-1	Summary of thirteen cases of subsurface jets in our data inventory.	11
4.1-1	CUPOM 1993-1999 products.	59
4.1-2	Model jet candidate summary.	60

ACRONYMS AND ABBREVIATIONS

ADCP	acoustic Doppler current profiler
AEF	Accurate Environmental Forecasting, Inc.
AT	Atwater Valley
AVHRR	advanced very high resolution radiometer satellite
BP	British Petroleum
CCAR	Colorado Center for Astrodynamics Research
CGS	coarse grid scale
COTR	Contracting Officer's Technical Representative
CTD	conductivity-temperature-depth sensors
CU	University of Colorado
CUPOM	CU implementation of the Princeton Ocean Model
DC	DeSoto Canyon
ECMWF	European Center for Mid-Range Weather Forecasting
EIS	DeSoto Canyon Eddy Intrusion Study
EW	Ewing Bank
FASINEX	Frontal Air-Sea Interaction Experiment
FGS	fine grid scale
GC	Green Canyon
LC	Loop Current
LCE	Loop Current Eddy
MC	Mississippi Canyon
MMS	Minerals Management Service
MRB	Model Review Board
NASA	National Aeronautics and Space Administration
NGDC	National Geophysical Data Center
NLOM	Navy Layered Ocean Model
NOAA	National Oceanic and Atmospheric Administration
NOGAPS	Navy Operation Global Atmospheric Prediction System
NOS	National Ocean Survey
NRL	Naval Research Laboratory
OCS	outer continental shelf
PG	percent good
PI	Principal Investigator or Port Isabel
PROFS	Princeton Regional Ocean Forecasting System
PV	potential vorticity
QA/QC	quality control and quality assurance
RDI	RD Instruments, Inc.
S	salinity
SAIC	Science Applications International Corporation
SSH	sea surface height
SST	sea surface temperature
T	temperature
TAMU	Texas A&M University
TLP	tension leg platform

ACRONYMS AND ABBREVIATIONS (continued)

USGS   United States Geological Survey
UTC   Universal time coordinated
V   velocity
VK   Viosca Knoll
XBT   expendable bathymetric thermograph

1. EXECUTIVE SUMMARY

The Minerals Management Service (MMS) of the U.S. Department of the Interior funded the Study of Subsurface High-Speed Current Jets in the Deep Water Region of the Gulf of Mexico (Jets). The contract was awarded to the Texas A&M Research Foundation on 22 September 1999, and the work was performed by Texas A&M University scientists Worth D. Nowlin, Jr., Program Manager, Steven F. DiMarco, Deputy Program Manager, Matthew K. Howard, Data Manager, and Robert O. Reid. The study objectives are to characterize known occurrences of high-speed, subsurface-intensified currents, known as jets, and to explore mechanisms responsible for their generation.

We have identified a total of 13 candidate cases of jets in our observational database. The candidate jets occur over a twelve-year period (1990-2001); this period is coincident with the period in which acoustic Doppler current profiler (ADCP) records have become available. Only profiling current meters possess the necessary vertical resolution to detect and measure a jet event. Based on observations, high-speed subsurface intensified currents typically have temporal durations on the order of a few hours to one day, have subsurface speed maxima that can exceed 4 knots (200 cm·s^{-1}), have peak speeds that occur between 150 and 350 m below the surface, and have little or no surface expressions. One of the jets consists of an inertial wave packet caused by Hurricane Georges that propagated downward to at least 500 m depth. Several of the observed jets have unusually large (> 10 cm·s^{-1}) vertical velocities, suggesting possible measurement error.

We have not ruled out the possibility that the measurement limitations of acoustical instruments may be responsible for certain biases in the data record. In particular, we have simulated a non-homogeneous flow field passing a realistic alignment of off-axis acoustic beams (typical of standard acoustic current instrumentation). We find that current inhomogeneities, both vertical and horizontal, can significantly affect the estimates of both horizontal and vertical current velocities. Further, for beam angles of 20°, oppositely directed vertical velocity components in each beam path can correspond to the appearance of horizontal velocities 2.74 times the vertical velocity magnitude. Such inhomogeneities could be caused by structural interference, internal waves, or motions attributed to ship/rig thrusters and could masquerade as energetic features in data records.

Although most of the observations of jets have serious instrumentation and data quality issues associated with the current measurements, there is sufficient evidence to assert that unusually high-speed and short-lived sub-surface current events exist.

We have obtained model outputs from two versions of the Princeton Ocean Model for the Gulf of Mexico: the Princeton Regional Ocean Forecasting System (PROFS) model (data courtesy L. Oey, Princeton University) and the University of Colorado Princeton Ocean Model (CUPOM) (data courtesy L. Kantha, University of Colorado). Four candidate jet events were identified in the CUPOM model output. They were in the vicinity of the twelve north-central Gulf of Mexico observational jet candidates and at comparable water depths and placement over the slope. Generally, all four of the CUPOM jet candidates could be associated with motions of filamentary structures extending from the Loop Current or eddies associated with the Loop Current. We believe the filaments are caused by the interaction of the Loop Current with bottom topography and/or eddy-eddy interaction. The temporal duration of the subsurface features found in the model were typically much longer (2-6 days or longer) than those seen in observations (one-third to 2 days). Also, the high-speed core (as large as 70 cm·s^{-1}) in the model was generally higher in the water column (150-250 m) than in observations (150-350 m).

Analysis of the coarse grid scale version of the PROFS model revealed no instances of intense sub-surface jets in the study region. However, there were several occurrences of isolated internal wave trains of inertial period. These wave trains, with peak speeds over 20 cm·s^{-1}, are likely associated with the passage of eddies.

Outputs of the Navy Layered Ocean Model during August of 1999 when an unusually large Loop Current Eddy (Eddy Juggernaut) was impinging on the north slopes show some filamentary structure in the region of interest.However, the subsurface motions between 200-300 m depth are generally accompanied with motions at the surface, which is inconsistent with subsurface jets (outputs courtesy T. Townsend of Naval Research Laboratory).

We should note the apparent disparity of time scales between jets observed in the real world and the jets found in the model output. The observed jets usually have time scales of the order of several hours to 1 day; we see no evidence in the model output of jets lasting less than one day. Model jets seem to occur higher in the water (not deeper than 200 m) and last 1-3 days.

Some candidate mechanisms seem more likely than others. The more likely mechanisms include: (a) motions derived from the Loop Current and associated eddies in the form of filaments and meanders, (b) motions due to eddy/eddy and/or slope-shelf/eddy interaction, (c) manifestations of internal waves with unusually large speeds, e.g. internal soliton, (d) the combined effects of transient surface winds and deep flow over an undulating sea bed, (e) reversed geostrophic flow, (f) inertial wave packets, and (g) frontal instabilities and the development of small-scale (15-25 km) preferentially cold-core features along frontal boundaries. Unlikely candidates (and reasons) include association with: coastal buoyancy fronts (too far from shore and river plume), upwelling (slower peak speeds and usually surface-trapped motions), and undercurrents (no evidence these exist in the Gulf of Mexico).

Recommendations are made regarding general oceanographic data collection as well as specific data collection strategies for capturing subsurface jets. The general recommendations include: the use of downward-looking long range (38 kHz) ADCPs on rigs, the routine collection of temperature and salinity profiles and meteorological data at such sites, the collection of near-bottom current data in deep water, the use of simple and portable acquisition system, regular backup and archival procedures for data, and the telemetry of data to a central onshore data facility. Recommendations specific to the detection and study of jets include: establish long term moored measurements in regions thought to contain jets, obtain temperature and salinity profiles during events, carry out targeted ship surveys during instability events (i.e., cyclone formation from eddy-topography interaction), and use standardized collection procedures. We recommend targeted field studies using moored instrumentation as well as ship surveys to capture jet events and provide evidence of their generation mechanisms and estimates of their spatial and temporal scales. Without such information, the real causes will remain questionable.

2. INTRODUCTION

2.1 Background and Program Objectives

There are four major classes of energetic currents in the Gulf of Mexico that are of primary importance to offshore petroleum operators. These are 1) currents resulting from energetic, episodic atmospheric events, 2) currents associated with the Loop Current and its related eddies, 3) vertically coherent currents below 1000 m (believed by some to be topographic Rossby waves), and 4) high-speed, subsurface-intensified currents.

The "Study of subsurface high-speed current jets in the deep water region of the Gulf of Mexico" (henceforth, "Jets Study" or "Study") seeks to characterize known jet occurrences and explore mechanisms responsible for their generation. The Study is a response to the observations by several deepwater petroleum operators of jets occurring over the upper continental slope of the northern Gulf of Mexico in water depths of about 1000 m and less. The Jets Study was one of four Gulf of Mexico numerical modeling studies funded by the Minerals Management Service in 1999. The three other studies involved analysis of full Gulf of Mexico numerical circulation models (Hamilton et al. 2003; Rothstein et al. 2003; Sturges et al., in press). Outputs of two of these studies were made available to this Study for analysis and interpretation; they are discussed in Sections 4.1 and 4.2.

The goals of the Jets Study are to:
- characterize the subsurface current jets that occur in the northern Gulf of Mexico, and
- identify and describe the physical mechanisms responsible for their generation.

Originally, eight activities were identified to achieve these goals. These activities governed the direction of the Jets Study until June 2001. During annual review meetings in May 2001 and January 2002, MMS and the MMS Model Review Board (MRB) amended these activities with other recommendations. The amendments were in response to the evolution of the Study's findings. The initial activities, with brief discussion of progress, are stated in the following paragraphs.

Identify and acquire data having subsurface current jets. This activity consists of an exhaustive search of our database for cases of subsurface current jets and the identification and acquisition of ancillary data sets that will aid in the interpretation of these jets. New sets of current data were identified as they became available during the course of this study.

Analyze data to characterize subsurface current jets. Each subsurface jet identified in our holdings was categorized by season, location, strength, vertical/horizontal (if available) profile, and duration. Once identified and categorized, our database was searched for concurrent measurements of current velocity, nearby CTD casts, and, where available, satellite images (SST, SSHA) to gain further insight to the cause, scale, and dynamics of the jet.

Prepare a climatology of subsurface current jet events. The goal of this task was to determine the frequency, location, and depth of occurrence; maximum speeds; duration and persistence; temporal/spatial scales; relation to topography; and dominant vertical pattern of these events.

3

Because of the rarity of observed jet events, the preparation of a climatology of jet events was abandoned in favor of additional numerical output analysis and generation mechanism speculation.

<u>Examine relationships between occurrence of jets and potential forcing phenomena.</u> The latter include documenting local presence of cyclonic or anticyclonic rings, interaction of rings with topography, formation of Loop Current eddies, and intense atmospheric events. We used extensive collateral data sets with which to examine these relationships, including sea surface height and sea surface temperature from satellites (1992 to present), drifter data from Gulf of Mexico dating from 1989, Horizon Marine Inc. Eddy Watch analyses, time series of Loop Current eddy formation from the Loop Current, and regional wind fields.

<u>Identify and analyze jets from numerical model output.</u> Initially, we used the University of Colorado's Princeton Ocean Model (CUPOM) high-resolution output for 1993-1999. We systematically examined the CUPOM output for cases of subsurface current jets. We then characterized the model jet events to examine the relation of the events to potential forcing phenomena seen in the model output. Insights gained from this activity were used to enhance and supplement the analyses of the observations. Numerical output from other circulation models became available during the course of the Study.

<u>Attempt identification of physical mechanisms responsible for generation of jets.</u> This activity was based on study of data and model output and of such phenomena reported in the literature. Onken (1990), for example, discusses the transformation that can occur within an oceanic frontal system (e.g., Loop Current, Gulf Stream, or eddies detached there from) by combined upwelling-downwelling at intermediate depths that cause a thermostad and hence reversal of geostrophic flow and a resulting low-frequency jet. The classical example of this mechanism is that associated with the submerged equatorial Cromwell Current. Another conceivable mechanism is the combined effects of transient surface winds and deep flow over an undulating sea bed that can cause downward and upward flux of energy to the water column at relatively high frequency, causing a subsurface baroclinic jet (Rhines 1977). Both mechanisms produce a divergence of flow in the subsurface regions, but at quite different frequencies of evolution. Yet both are baroclinic, in that they require strong density stratification

<u>Meetings with MMS and industry representatives.</u> Industry has a cadre of knowledgeable scientists who have studied the currents in the Gulf and their impact on industry operations. The goal of this activity was to identify additional pertinent data sets, present significant results, discuss ideas about the mechanisms that may generate the subsurface current jets, and exchange information and concepts on subsurface current jets. We participated in relevant Industry Workshops during the course of the Study.

<u>Synthesize results and prepare reports.</u> Dissemination of Study findings to interested parties (including MMS) was critical to the overall success of this study. We found that as the Study progressed and findings were made available, industry was more willing to cooperate with the Study and allow its participants access to proprietary industry data sets.

At the Annual Review Meetings of the MMS Gulf Numerical Studies held in Kenner, LA on May 8-9, 2001, and January 12-13, 2002, MMS representatives and the MRB made several recommendations to aid in direction and focus of the Study. The combined recommendations from these meetings are:

1. To provide guidance to MMS as to how data collection should be improved on oil and gas industry platforms.

2. To apply analysis schemes to the Princeton Regional Ocean Forecasting System (PROFS) model data outputs run both with and without assimilation. Outputs from two version of the model were collected: coarse grid scale (CGS) and fine grid scale (FGS). Dr. Leo Oey of Princeton University contributed outputs.

3. To use CUPOM model outputs to establish time-space scales of jets.

4. To continue to collect relevant observations as they become available.

5. To offer guesses as to causal mechanisms of subsurface jets *even if we are not sure.*

6. To take a close look at inertial/internal mechanisms for jet generation using the highest possible temporal and spatial resolution available (preferably hourly). In addition, attention should be paid to filamentary structure mechanisms for jet generation.

2.2 Definition of Subsurface Jet

To facilitate the identification of subsurface jet events in our observational and numerical model output databases, we established the following definition of high-speed subsurface intensified currents, or jets. Jets typically have temporal durations of a few hours to one day, have subsurface speed maxima that can exceed 4 knots (200 cm·s^{-1}), but are at least 40 cm·s^{-1}, have peak speeds that occur between 150-350 m below the sea surface, and have little or no energetic surface expression.

2.3 Importance to MMS and Offshore Industry

Currents at all depths are important factors for the transport of pollutants and other substances, including oil. Therefore, offshore operators design drilling and production systems to account for forces exerted by these currents (Farrant and Javed, 2001). Because several deepwater petroleum operators have reported cases of unusually high-speed subsurface-intensified currents that have disrupted, suspended, or delayed platform operations, the frequency, persistence, and speed characteristics of jets are important design criteria to reduce down time and to compensate for potential hazards like riser and tendon fatigue due to vortex induced vibration (VIV). It has been estimated that a 200 cm·s^{-1} jet event with a sheared unidirectional current profile will use up the fatigue life of a TLP tendon on the order of one week (Cort Cooper, personal communication). Further, knowledge of the occurrence of subsurface current jets can be important considerations for oil spill trajectory analysis and modeling, including spills from the deep seafloor.

The occurrence of subsurface jets can be important in the skill assessment of models. The observations suggest that there is a substantial vertical component of velocity associated with some jet events. Many of the full Gulf of Mexico numerical models used by MMS and industry assume the hydrostatic approximation, i.e., negligible vertical acceleration. If the observed large changes in vertical velocity on short time scales are validated, then MMS and industry must consider non-hydrostatic models for the Gulf of Mexico in the future.

2.4 Data and Output Descriptions

As part of our previous MMS studies and Texas A&M University's 50-year involvement in Gulf of Mexico research, we have assembled an extensive oceanographic database. Much of this data set was collected, quality controlled, analyzed, and archived for the MMS-funded Deepwater Physical Oceanography Reanalysis and Synthesis (Deepwater) Project (Nowlin et al. 2001). Our data set comprises virtually all of the publicly available current meter records from the Gulf of Mexico.

In addition to publicly available records, we have acquired many additional moored current meter and ADCP records from the offshore petroleum production industry. These current meter records are mostly from locations in U.S waters over the continental slope and rise of the north-central Gulf of Mexico where drilling pressures are greatest, although we also possess records from the western Gulf of Mexico. These records and assorted hydrographic data collections generally cover the time period from 1980 through 2001. We are confident that we have assembled the most comprehensive data set possible for this project.

Email was sent periodically during the Study to industry representatives, who owned proprietary or publicly available current meter data sets thought to contain jets, to solicit access to newly acquired current meter data or collateral survey (particularly hydrographic) data that may have been done concurrently with the current meter collection. The survey data were sought to more fully describe the general oceanographic conditions in the Gulf of Mexico during the time of the events and to investigate possible causal mechanisms. All contacted industry representatives responded to our request; although our requests yielded a few new current meter records, no hydrographic data were collected in the vicinity and time of the jets requested. The lack of temperature and salinity structure during jet events greatly lowered our ability to select the most likely mechanisms for jet generation.

The short temporal character and confined, relatively narrow vertical extent of jets provide a challenge to researchers attempting to investigate them. Because of the large vertical separation of moored single-point current meters (usually hundreds of meters), practically all current-meter data collected prior to 1990 are useless for the investigation of jets. With the advent of profiling acoustic current sensors, investigators were afforded the opportunity to collect profiles of current velocity with good vertical resolution (order several meters) over vertical ranges of tens to hundreds of meters. However, a single current profiler looking vertically through the water column does not provide any indication of the horizontal scale and structure of these jets. Unfortunately, there have been no deployments of multiple current profilers in the Gulf of Mexico in the depth range of the water column when jets occurred. Therefore, there is no direct observational data on which to quantitatively investigate the horizontal scales of jets.

Most industry records containing jet events were produced when suspending an ADCP from a drill ship or other platform. Unfortunately, much of the documentation (metadata) regarding these industry-sponsored records is missing or inadequate to allow complete understanding of the mooring configurations. Further, the data itself were sometimes in less than desirable formats including: paper copies of plotted data or digital images of computer screens containing current meter data.

In addition to in situ current meter and hydrographic data, we also collected available satellite derived altimetry and AVHRR sea surface temperature products. The altimetry products were collected mostly from the Colorado Center for Astrodynamics Research through Dr. Robert Leben's interactive website (http://www-ccar.colorado.edu/research/gom/html/gom_nrt.html) but also as a specialized altimetry product provided to us for use in the MMS-funded Northeast Gulf of Mexico Chemical Oceanography and Hydrography Study (Jochens et al. 2002). The altimetry data basically covered the period from April 1992 through December 2002. The sea surface height fields derived from the satellite altimetry uses a combination of altimeter data from TOPEX/Poseidon and ERS-2 satellites with 10-day and 35-day repeat orbits, respectively. See Jochens et al. (2002) for more information on altimeter products.

Sea surface temperature products were obtained using the Johns Hopkins University Applied Physics Laboratory Ocean Remote Sensing website (http://fermi.jhuapl.edu/avhrr/gm/index.html). Available are 3-day and 7-day image composites of Advanced Very High Resolution Radiometer from April 1996 to December 2002 (and beyond).

We also have acquired for this study 3 CD-ROMs (Volumes 3, 4, & 5) from NOAA's National Geophysical Data Center (NGDC) that contain their newly released Coastal Relief Gridded Database series for the US Gulf of Mexico. These constitute a merger of the USGS Digital Elevation Model (DEM) for the US Gulf coastal states with the best available bathymetric data sets from the National Ocean Survey (NOS) and university sources. Marine coverage is essentially the US EEZ. The data are gridded at a horizontal resolution of approximately 90 m with a vertical resolution of 0.10 m. See http://www.ngdc.noaa.gov/mgg/coastal/coastal.html for complete details on the regional coverage, data sources, and data assembly methodology. We have modified software supplied by NGDC to run on our workstations. The software allows us to read the NGDC format and extract detailed bathymetry for our areas of interest.

Other ancillary data include various wind products (time series from NDBC buoys, coastal regional airports and gridded model wind products, including ETA and ECMWF) and river discharge time series from gauging stations of major rivers of the northern Gulf of Mexico. The ancillary data sets were collected early in the Study, but were of limited use for interpreting subsurface jets. We include them here for completeness; but will not discuss them further.

Because of the relative paucity of deepwater current data, we supplemented the observational data with the output of several numerical circulation models. The initial model examined was provided to us courtesy of Drs. Lakshmi Kantha and Jei-Kook Choi at CCAR. Their model, the University of Colorado Princeton Ocean Model (CUPOM), is a modified version of the Princeton Ocean Model having an improved surface boundary layer (Kantha et al. 1999). It is a sigma coordinate model with 21 depths and 1/12° horizontal resolution. Forcing is by upstream boundary conditions that simulate the Loop Current, by surface wind stress fields from atmospheric models, and by air-sea fluxes. It is constrained by assimilating satellite-derived sea surface height and sea surface temperature. The model assimilates SSH through the construction of pseudo-temperature profiles which when combined with historical temperature-salinity relationships yield a water column of height that matches the observed SSH. The model outputs temperature, salinity, and two components of horizontal velocity. The version of the model available to us and subsequent runs of this model are actively used by industry and MMS for simulating mesoscale features in the Gulf of Mexico, and is operated quasi-operationally to obtain nowcasts and forecasts of the Gulf. Initially, we used results from a 6-year simulation (1993-1999) that was also available to the Deepwater Study. Nowlin et al. (2001) describes the model products available to the Study for analysis. A second run of the CUPOM covering the same temporal period as the first run was also made available to the Study in December 2001. The two sets of output form a complementary set which were made available to the JETS study.

Model outputs were obtained from three separate runs of the Princeton Regional Ocean Forecast System (PROFS) Princeton Ocean Model of Dr. Leo Oey of Princeton University. All three runs of the model had 26 sigma-layers in the vertical. Available to us were two runs of the coarse grid scale (CGS) version that covered the time period from January 1997 through December 1999. One of the CGS runs was with data assimilation; the other was not. Output of the CGS run were available only at selected locations in the Gulf of Mexico (probe locations) and at at 3-hourly intervals. Figure 2.4-1 shows the locations of the PROFS CGS probe locations. An additional run using the fine grid scale (FGS) version of the non-assimilated model covering a 90-day period from August 1998 through October 1998 was also available. For more information on the PROFS model see Hamilton et al. (2003). The horizontal grid size of the PROFS CGS model varies from about 10 km (near the Loop Current) to about 5 km in the northern Gulf. The grid size for the FGS version is about one-half that of the CGS version. Model output is at discrete isolated points, i.e., pseudo-probe locations rather than at a fully dense grid. Figure 2.4-2 shows the grid where PROFS FGS output was made available for this study.

2.5 Report Organization

Section 3 presents descriptions of the jet events found in current meter observations. This section also summarizes limitations of current measurement using multiple beam acoustic Doppler profiling instruments. Section 4 presents descriptions and interpretations of jet events found in several different numerical models. Section 5 discusses the plausible and implausible mechanisms of jet generation. Section 6 presents recommendations for oceanographic data collection aboard offshore drilling and production platforms. Section 7 summarizes the conclusions of this study and offers suggestions for further investigations and lines of inquiry.

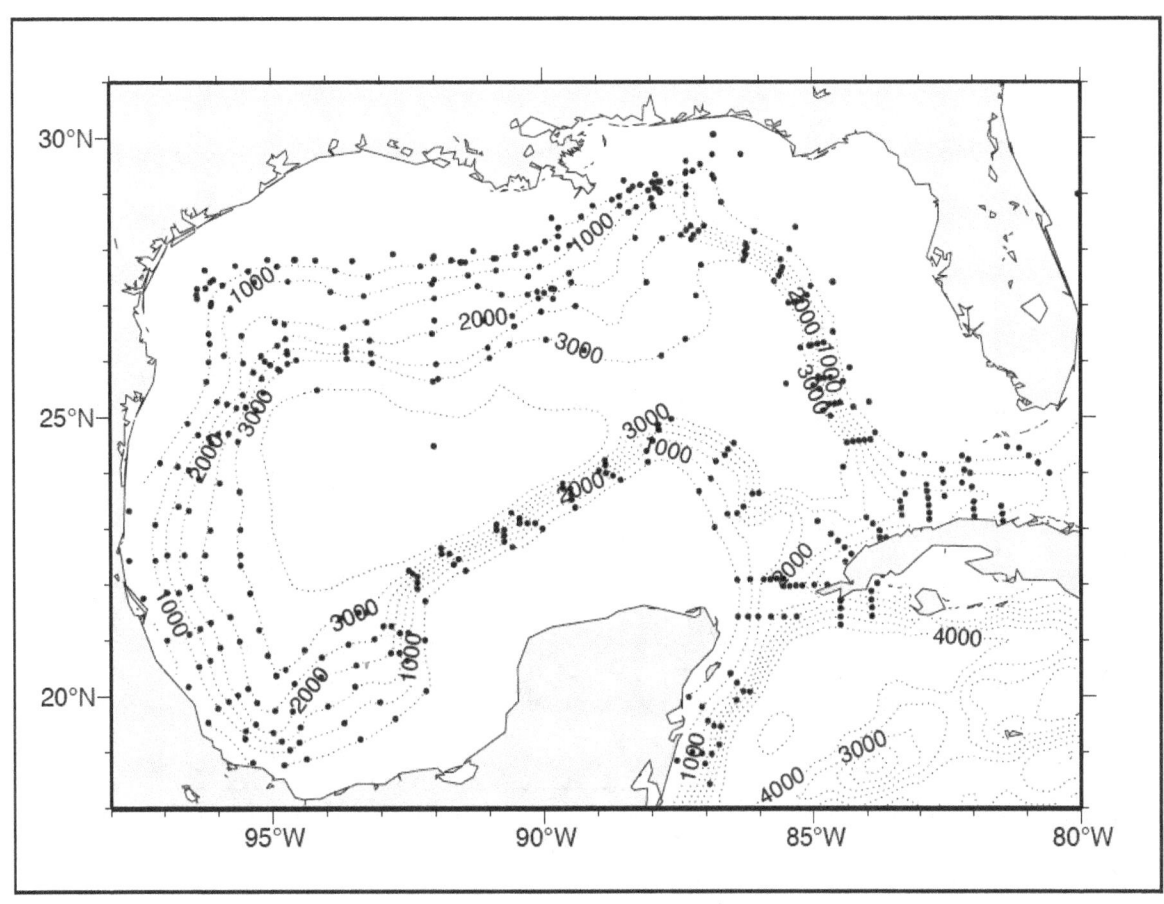

Figure 2.4-1. PROFS model probe locations (dots) in the Gulf of Mexico. Isobaths shown are 500, 1000, 1500, 2000, 2500, 3000, and 3500 m. [Figure courtesy L. Oey, Princeton University.]

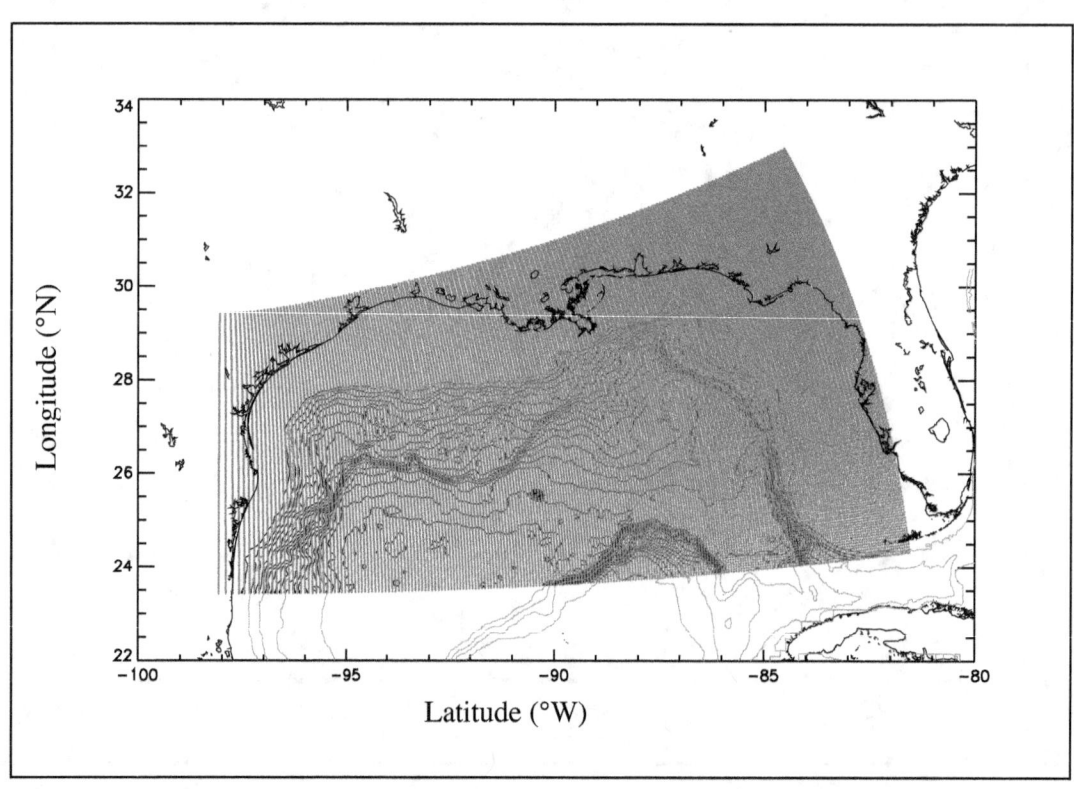

Figure 2.4-2. The Gulf of Mexico subdomain of Leo Oey's PROFS FGS model. Grid is 240 X 289 X 25 shown in red, model bathymetry is shown in gray, Herring bathymetry in green and the GMT coastline.

10

3. OBSERVATIONS

3.1 Descriptions of Jet Candidates

Table 3.1-1 summarizes the locations, dates, and maximum speeds of the thirteen jets contained in proprietary and non-proprietary current meter records. Two of the jets listed in this table (jets 4 and 13) are from confidential industry data sets: they are only identified by year and lease region. The five jets whose status is listed as "Restricted" are from proprietary industry data sets as well; however, permission has been granted from the data owners to allow their quantitative description and display in this report. When the total water depth was unknown, a nominal depth for the lease block is reported.

Table 3.1-1. Summary of Thirteen Cases of Subsurface Jet Currently in Our Data Inventory.

No.	LB	DATE	LON	LAT	Data Status	J-Depth	Max. Spd	T-Depth
			°W	°N		m	cm·s⁻¹	m
1.	MC72	19 Apr 1990	88.587	28.910	Restricted	300	150+	1000
2.	GC200	30 Apr 1994	90.749	27.767	Unrestricted	210	60+	600
3.	AT575	16 Jul 1995	89.785	27.366	Restricted	175	50+	2000
4.	PI	1996			Confidential			
5.	VK956	10 Feb 1997	88.094	29.045	Unrestricted	275	105+	1200
6.	MC628	10 Apr 1997	89.366	28.332	Unrestricted	325	80+	760
7.	GC505	04 Nov 1997	90.902	27.465	Restricted	225	40+	1306
8.	GC505	20 Nov 1997	90.902	27.465	Restricted	225	60+	1306
9.	GC236	09 Apr 1998	91.142	27.730	Unrestricted	180	60+	600
10.	DC977	28 Sep 1998	87.494	28.003	Unrestricted	Unknown	25+	1300
11.	GC506	25 Oct 1998	90.853	27.464	Restricted	275	60+	1295
12.	EW913	16 Aug 1999	90.399	28.066	Unrestricted	160	210+	500
13.	GC	2001			Confidential			

J-Depth is depth of jet core.　　　T-Depth is total water depth.　　　Max. Spd is maximum jet speed.

Figure 3.1-1 shows the locations of the eleven unrestricted and restricted candidate jets. Observation locations are labeled by the lease block in which they occur. We see that most of the known jet occurrences are confined to the slope regions of the north-central Gulf of Mexico. However, this region also coincides with the highest density of observations from offshore operations. One jet is located in the western Gulf of Mexico in Lease Region Port Isabel (PI).

Eleven of the thirteen jets listed in Table 3.1-1 are from ADCP instruments (jets 2-9, and 11-13). Jet number 1 was measured using a lowered InterOcean S4 current meter and Jet 10 was measured with a combination of an upward-looking ADCP and conventional rotor-type current meters. The ADCP quality parameter "percent good" was available for all of these jets except jet 10. Of the seven remaining jets where percent good is available, only two jets (numbers 3 and 6) did not show a significant drop in "percent good" at the depth and time of the jet occurrence.

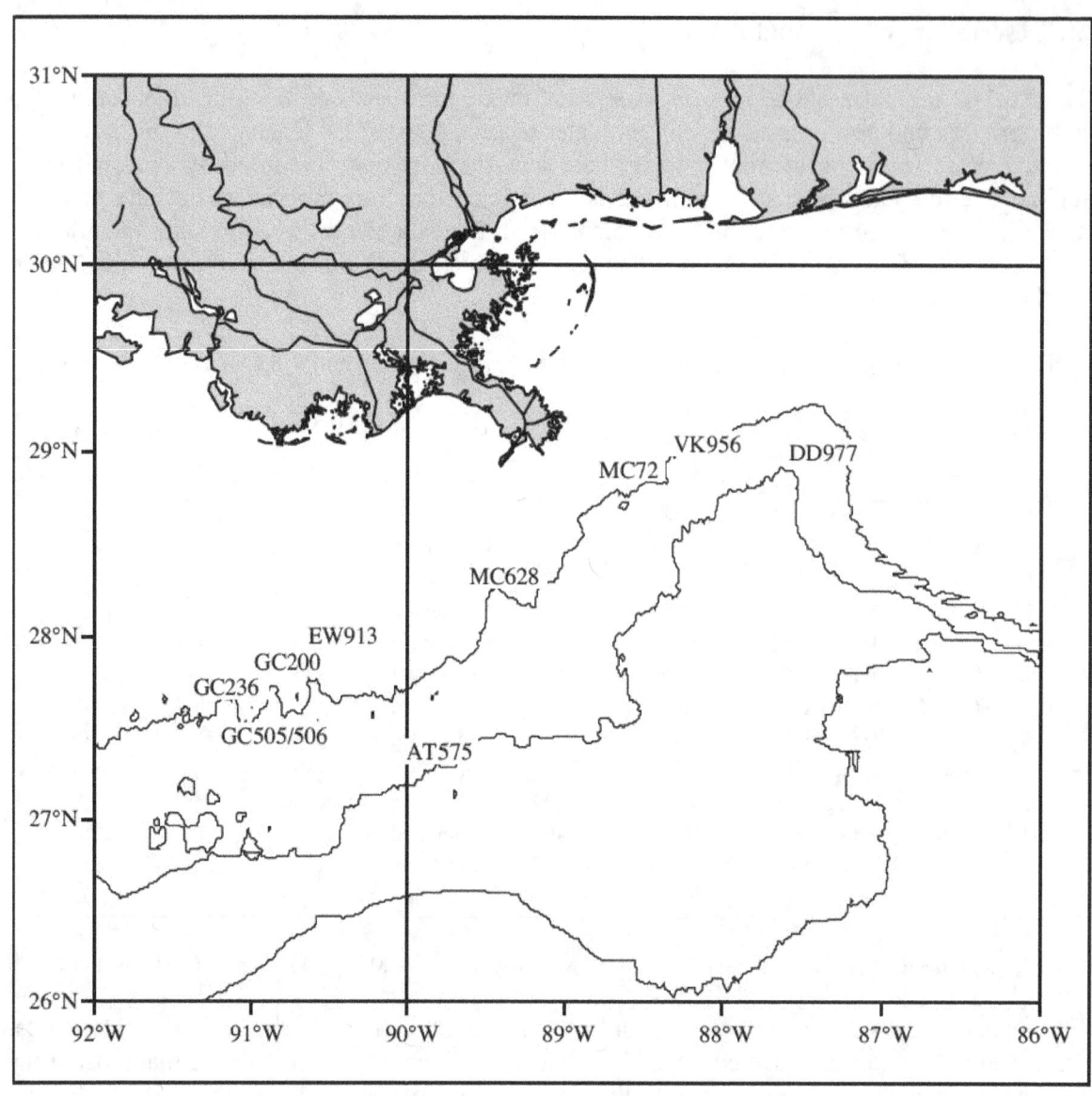

Figure 3.1-1. Locations of candidate occurrences of mid-depth current jets in the Gulf of Mexico from public and restricted current observational data sets (see Table 2.5-1). Isobaths shown are 1000, 2000, and 3000 m. Jets are labeled by lease block. Center of label is jet location.

Because a sudden and abrupt decrease in percent good can indicate a decrease in data quality, we contacted the ADCP manufacturer, RDI, for guidance on how to interpret these data. RDI indicated that among the factors that can produce spurious measurements are large thermal gradients, unusually large tilt values, and heterogeneous scatterer concentration. Further, RDI has indicated that beam refraction can play a role in producing unusually large vertical velocities, which have been seen in the observations. Most seriously, however, the violation of the homogeneous flow assumption can significantly affect current estimates. This will be discussed more in Section 3.2.

We now present short narrative descriptions of each of the candidate jet events listed in Table 3.1-1. These narrative descriptions include descriptions based on collateral data of potential forcing phenomena, such as atmospheric storms and oceanic eddies, that may be responsible for the occurrence of the jets. Illustrations of currents, sea surface temperature, and sea surface altimetry are provided when available. The eleven non-confidential jets are described here.

3.1.1   MC72: 19 April 1990

In early April 1990, an oil-drilling platform owned by BP experienced usually large sub-surface currents during drilling operations. The platform was forced to suspend operations until currents returned to safe and acceptable speeds for drilling. Additionally, the event was unusual because there was no surface expression of the subsurface currents. Several days later, current meter instrumentation was deployed in Mississippi Canyon Lease Block 72 in an effort to quantify the vertical structure of current speed at this location. An InterOcean S4 electromagnetic current meter was deployed at varying intervals (6 to 10 hours) beginning 15 April 1990 and ending 19 May 1990. The S4 was simply suspended by a line to the surface and lowered at roughly 100-foot (30.5 m) increments to 2000 feet (610 m). The instrument was free to swing and spin on the lowering line during the deployment. Beginning on April 30, an Aanderaa current meter was occasionally lowered with the S4. According to Horizon Marine's Eddy Watch chart for that period, the Loop Current was well south of the instrument. However, a warm circulation feature was intruding from the Loop Current into the DeSoto Canyon. This feature appears to be in the vicinity of the platform.

Currents in the upper 150 m were weak and generally less than 20 cm·s⁻¹ throughout the deployment. From April 15-17, currents below 150 m were more variable with speeds from 20-80 cm·s⁻¹ and with current direction covering the full compass range, 0-360°. On 18 April 0900 UTC, a subsurface jet appeared between 150 and 400 m depth; current speed exceeded 150 cm·s⁻¹ at 300 m. There is no indication of the jet eight hours before (0100 UTC) or after (1700 UTC). On 19 April 0100 UTC, the jet reappeared between 150 and 450 m; speeds exceeded 170 cm·s⁻¹ (Figure 3.1.1-1). Current speed directions at this time and depth range from 60° to 350°. At 1100 UTC, the jet is again seen at the same depths with similar speeds. By 1700 UTC, currents returned to speeds less than 40 cm·s⁻¹ throughout the water column.

On 21 April 0745 and 1550 UTC, currents showed very strong vertical shear, going from 5 cm·s⁻¹ to 160 cm·s⁻¹ over 30 m. The speed core was spatially narrower than before—only 75-150 m thick. From 22-24 April, speeds between 300 and 450 m occasionally peaked to more than

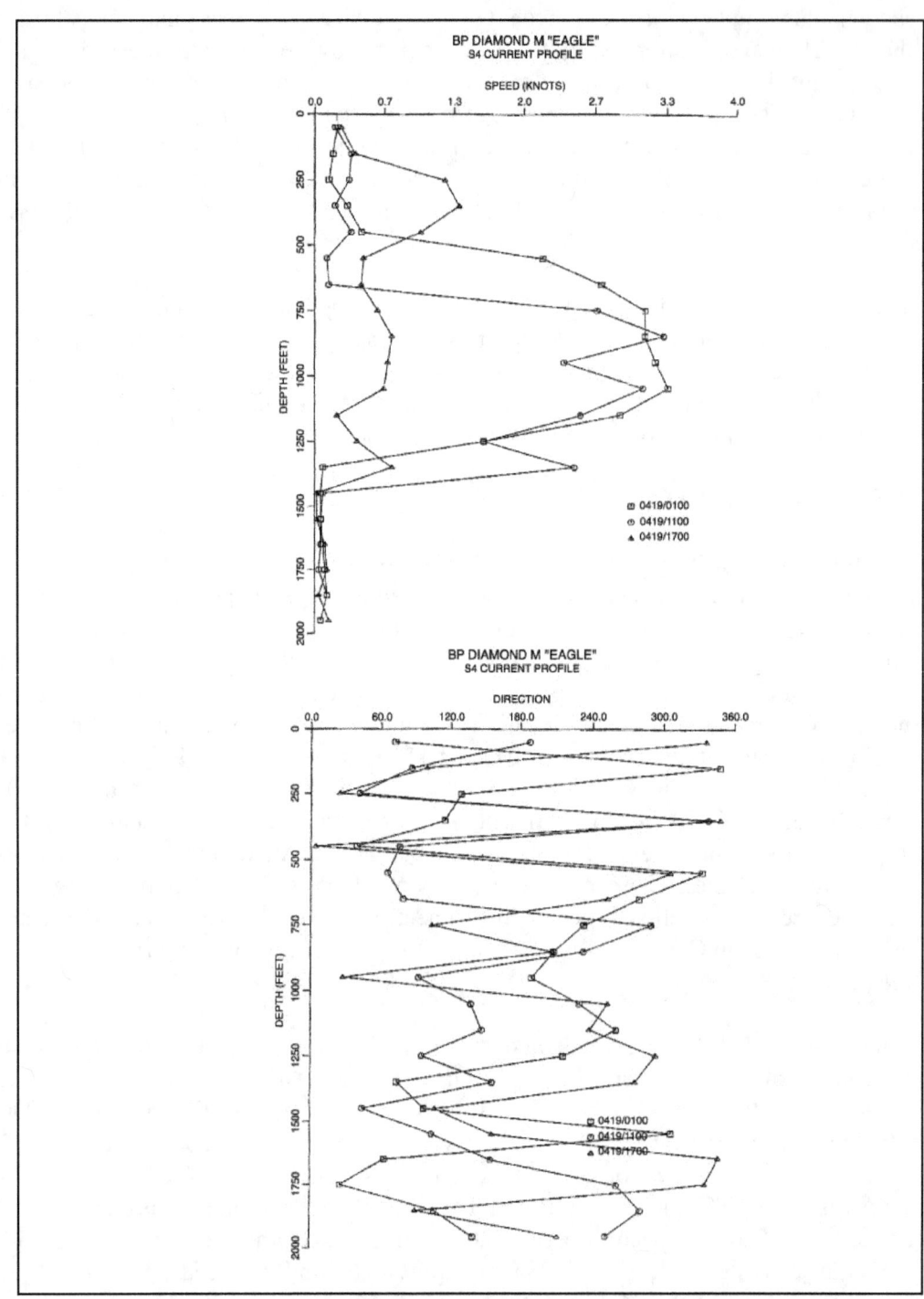

Figure 3.1.1-1. Profiles of current speed (top) and direction (bottom) from lowered S4 current meter at lease block MC72 during jet event on 19 April 1990. Times of profiles are 0100, 1100, and 1700 UTC. Note English measurement units.

100 cm·s^{-1}, while the current between the surface and 300 m generally was below 25 cm·s^{-1}. After 25 April until the end of deployments on 19 May, currents rarely exceed 20 cm·s^{-1} at any depth. Further, there was very good agreement for speed and direction between the simultaneously lowered S4 and Aanderaa instruments although the simultaneous lowering of these instruments only occurred during the quiescent periods.

This is the first observational record of a subsurface jet event in the Gulf of Mexico. Unfortunately, the instrument was first deployed only several days after the first current event. The data during the subsequent events are considered somewhat suspect because the instrument was allowed to swing freely. Also, the extremely large shear and widely varying directional changes, which occurred over short vertical distances and short time periods, also cast doubt on the validity on these measurements.

3.1.2 Jet 2 in GC200: 30 April 1994

The second candidate jet in the database occurred 30 April 1994. Figure 3.1.2-1 (top) shows speed contours during this jet. Data are courtesy of Marathon Oil Company. The 75-kHz ADCP data were taken at four-minute intervals and binned into eight-meter bins. The sampling rate for this record is high compared to that in most other data sets examined–generally every 30 minutes or more. This jet propagated upward in time with peak speeds greater than 50 cm·s^{-1} at about 210 m depth. The jet lasted on the order of eight hours. The raw speeds have been smoothed with a 25-point boxcar filter to stabilize the contouring. Figure 3.1.2-1 (bottom) shows contours of percent good during the same time period. The raw percent good values were smoothed with a 25-point boxcar filter prior to contouring. The most notable feature of this plot is the band of low percent good between 110- to 180-m depth. Negative percent good indicates that no usable data were available. This band most likely represents interference by part of the drill ship structure with the acoustic pulse. The plot also shows a decrease of percent good at the far limits of the instrument range. In this case, it is below 400-m depth. During the jet, however, a distinct decrease in percent good occurred following the upward propagating signal. Raw percent good values during the jet were as low as 60. The sudden decrease in percent good casts some doubt on the validity of this jet. Further, it is possible that the structural interference between 110 and 180 m prevented the observation of energetic phenomena at those depths.

SSH during the period of this jet (Figure 3.1.2-2) showed a weak (5.0 cm maximum height) elongated anticyclone centered south of the DeSoto Slope. The ADCP was located north and west of two strong cyclonic features. A Loop Current Eddy (Eddy Creole) was well to the south, centered at 89°W, 25°N. The Loop Current did not extend north of 27°N. AVHRR sea surface temperature imagery (not shown) revealed a weak atmospheric cold front passing through the region at about the time of the jet. It is unclear whether the presence of this front influenced the currents at depth. We note that the sea temperature at the depth of the ADCP remained steady at about 23°C during the time of the jet, while temperature fluctuations of about 2°C were present for several days before and after the event.

This jet event was contained in a much longer record that spanned 14 February 1994 through 2 June 1994. In general, the record was noisy, with many velocity outliers (isolated or single-point measurements outside statistical limits of what is expected based on the record's characteristics).

15

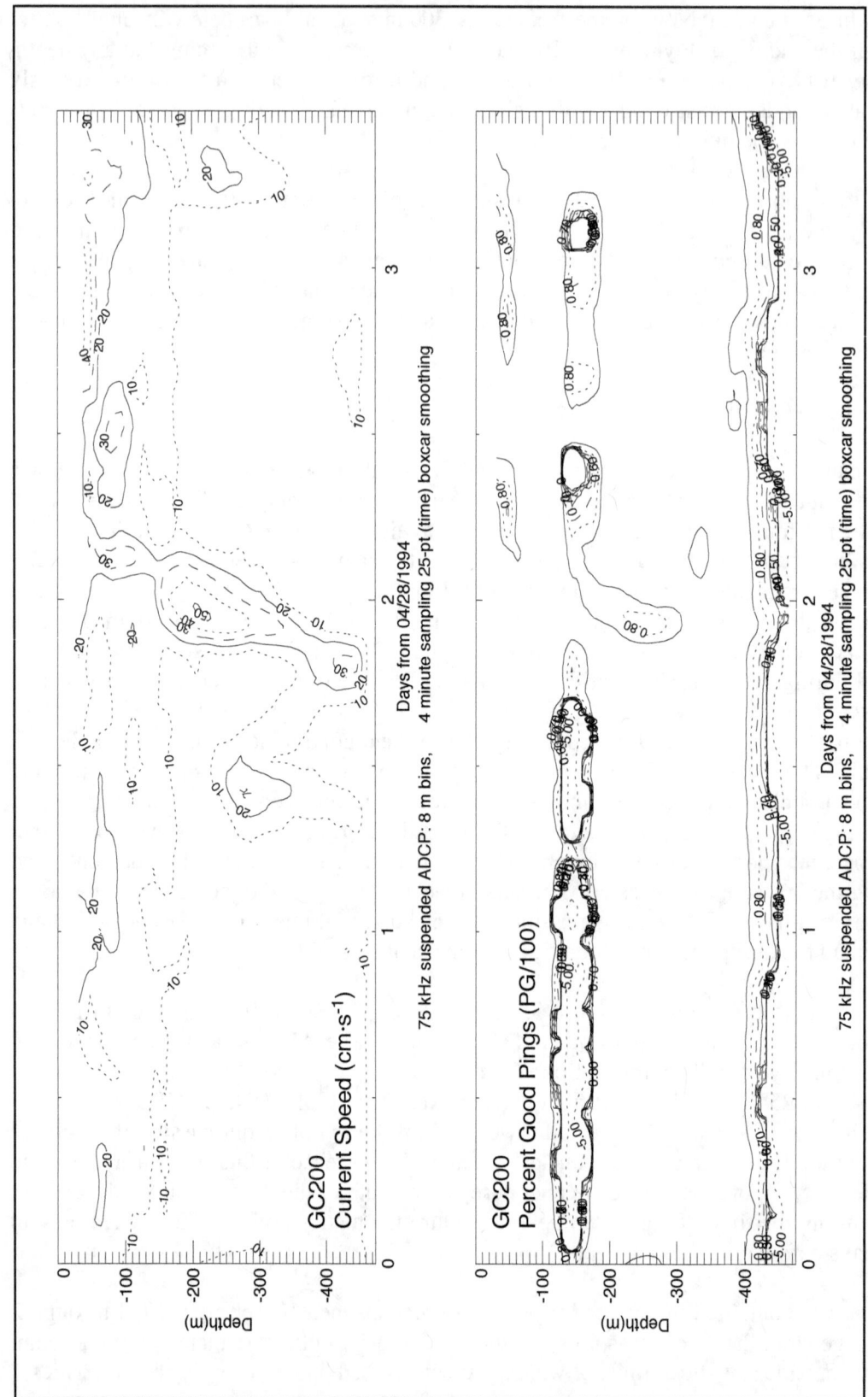

Figure 3.1.2-1. Top: Contours of current speed versus depth and time showing subsurface jet occurring in lease block GC200 during 29 April 1994. Contour interval is 10 cm·s⁻¹. Bottom: Contours of percentage of good pings per sampling ensemble versus depth and time at same time and location as top panel. Data courtesy Marathon Oil Company.

16

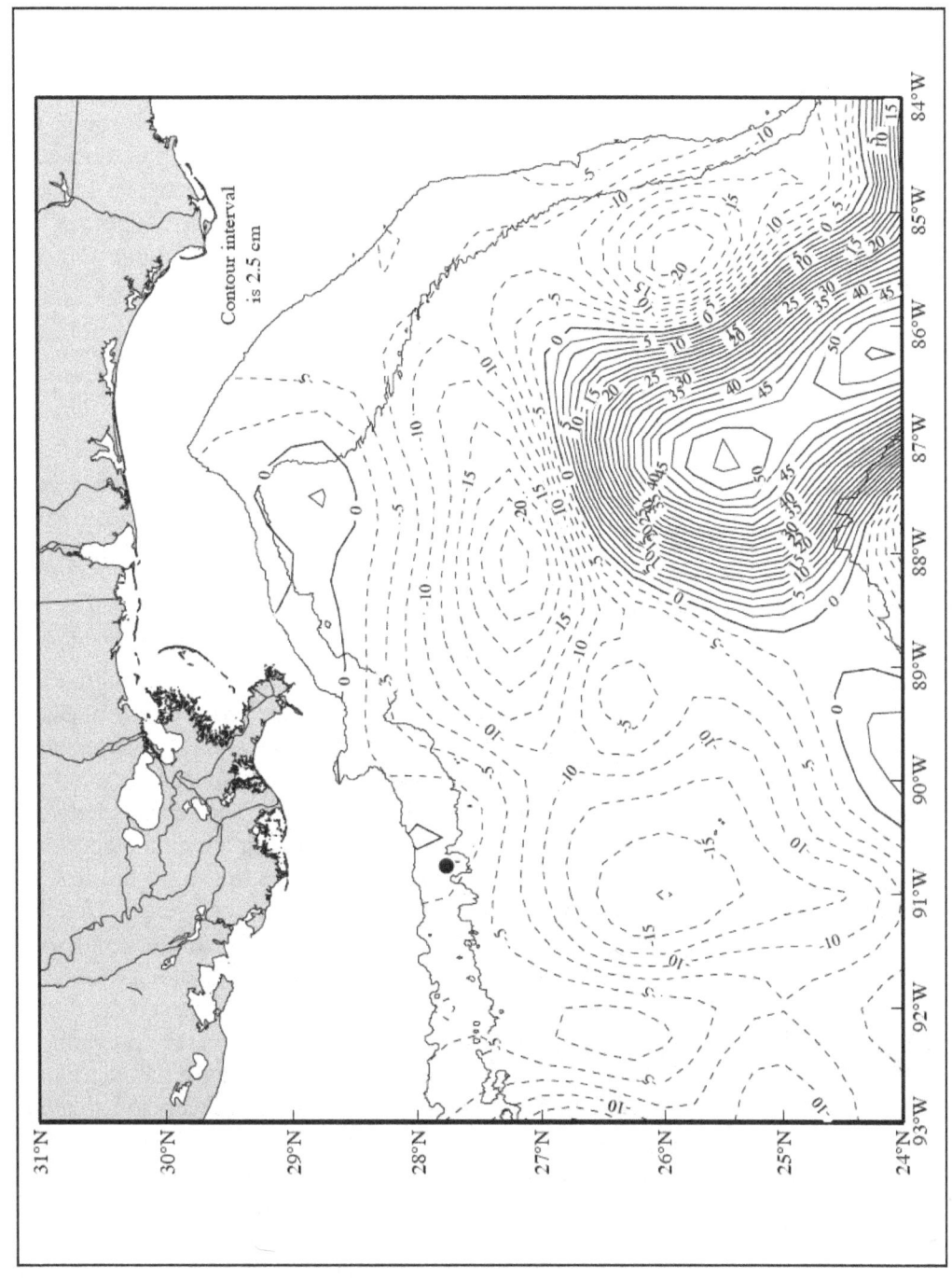

Figure 3.1.2-2. Sea-surface height field from satellite altimeter data for 30 April 1994 for GC200 case. The 200 and 100-m isobath contours are shown. [Data provided by Robert R. Leben, University of Colorado; plot provided courtesy of Ann Jochens, TAMU].

17

3.1.3   Jet 3 in AT575: 16 July 1995

On 2 April 1995, Woods Hole Group deployed a 75-kHz ADCP on a drill ship in roughly 2000 m water depth in Atwater Valley Lease Block 575. Data are courtesy of BP/Amoco. The deployment was for routine monitoring of ocean current during drilling operations. The deployment ended 5 November 1995. Measurements were taken at 20 minute intervals using 8 m depth bins. During the deployment a Loop Current Eddy (Eddy Zapp) passed through the location causing near-surface current speed in excess of 100 cm·s^{-1}. As the trailing eastern edge of the eddy passed the instrument's location on 16 July 1995, a jet appeared between 150 and 200 m with maximum speed of about 55 cm·s^{-1} and lasted on the order of one day (Figure 3.1.3-1). The SSH field about the time of this jet clearly showed the location of the compact and intense LCE (SSH > 30 cm) relative to the drill ship (Figure 3.1.3-2).

Vertical and error velocity fields were not available to us during this deployment. Contours of the percentage of good pings during each measurement do not show any indication of data quality reduction during the time and depth of the jet (Figure 3.1.3-3).

Generally, this record is considered of good quality. However, following the jet event the record contains several large gaps presumably when the instrument was turned off during repositioning or relocation of the drill ship.

3.1.4   Jet 5 in VK956: 10 February 1997

A total of 111 profiles of current velocity were measured in lease block VK956 using an RD Instruments 75 kHz narrowband ADCP during 10-11 February 1997. Data are courtesy of Shell. The time interval between the beginnings of each profile was 10 minutes. Data were collected in 17-m bins from 46 m below the surface to 500 m below surface. Current speeds between the surface and 200 m remained relatively unchanged during the deployment with speeds between 15 and 25 cm·s^{-1} (Figure 3.1.4-1). The development of a sub-surface jet with maximum speeds of 105 cm·s^{-1} at 300 m depth and lasting roughly six hours can be followed through the first 50 profiles. The jet is not seen eight hours (roughly 60 profiles) after the occurrence. Detailed analysis of these data included plotting and analyzing the percentage of good pings during each profile, (each profile is an average of many pings), the measured vertical velocity, and the measured error velocity. The ADCP purposely had one of its four transducers turned off during this deployment because it pointed directly at the platform riser. This, however, prevents an estimate of error velocity. Moreover, it decreases the overall data quality because the instrument can no longer use the four-beam algorithm to estimate current velocity and must resort to a less accurate three-beam solution. Analysis of percent good during the event shows a slight decrease when the jet is at its maximum speed. Estimates of vertical velocity exceeded 20 cm·s^{-1} between 200 and 500 m depth during the event, but were near zero before and after the event (Figure 3.1.4-2). This feature has been observed in other jets as well. After inspection of the raw data files, RDI engineers have indicated there is no apparent instrument malfunction and, from an instrumentation perspective, the data appear good. Figure 3.1.4-3 shows the sea surface height of the eastern Gulf of Mexico during the jet event. A weak slope anticyclone was present south of the measurement location. The Loop Current and a separated LCE (Eddy Creole) was well to the

18

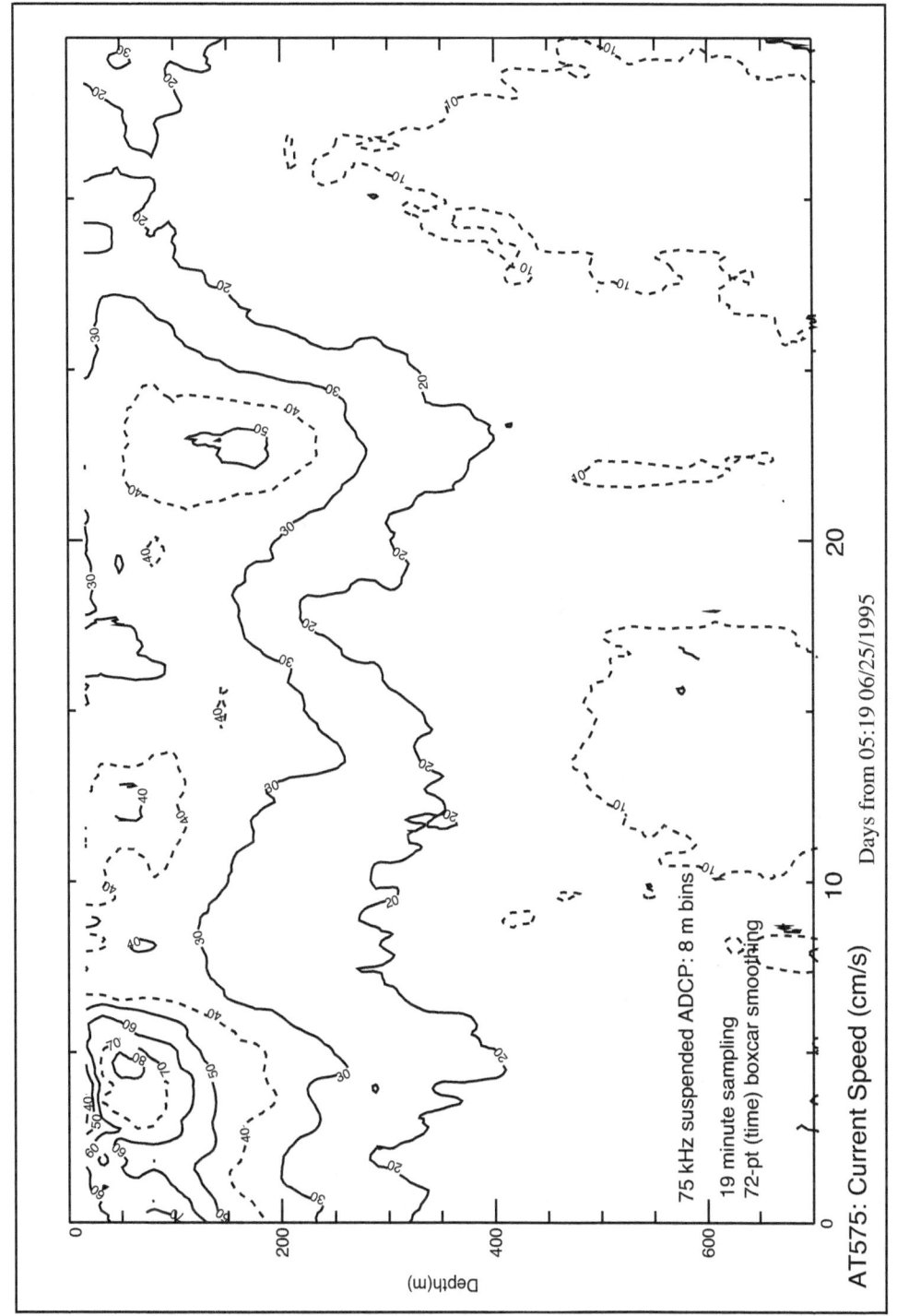

Figure 3.1.3-1. Contours of current speed versus depth and time showing subsurface jet occurring in lease block AT575. Contour interval is 10 cm/s; data are in 8 m bins and 19 minute sampling interval. Data are courtesy BP.

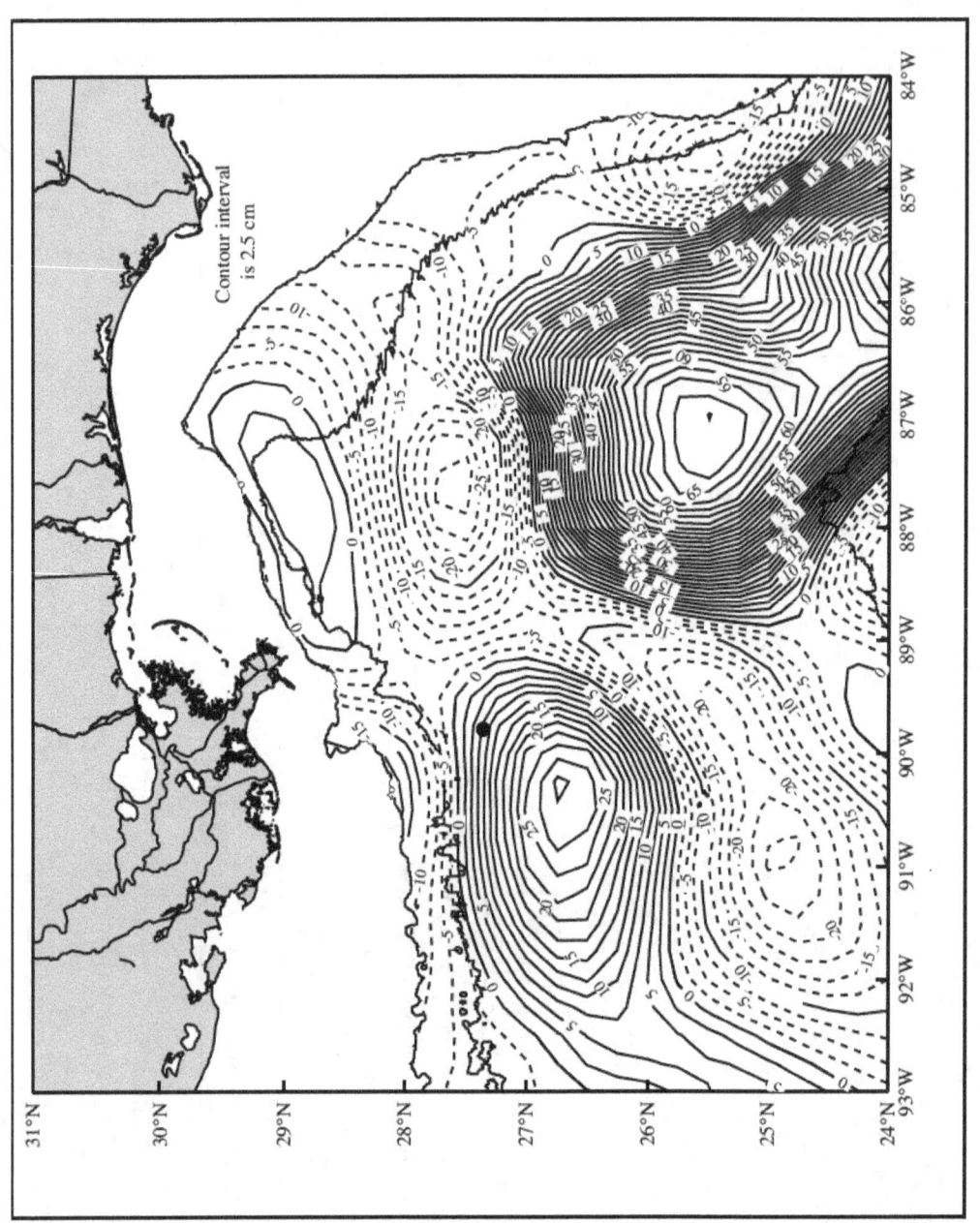

Figure 3.1.3-2. Sea-surface height field from satellite altimeter data for 6 July 1995 for AT575 case (dot). The 200 and 1000-m isobath contours are shown. [Data provided by Robert R. Leben, University of Colorado; plot is courtesy of Ann Jochens.]

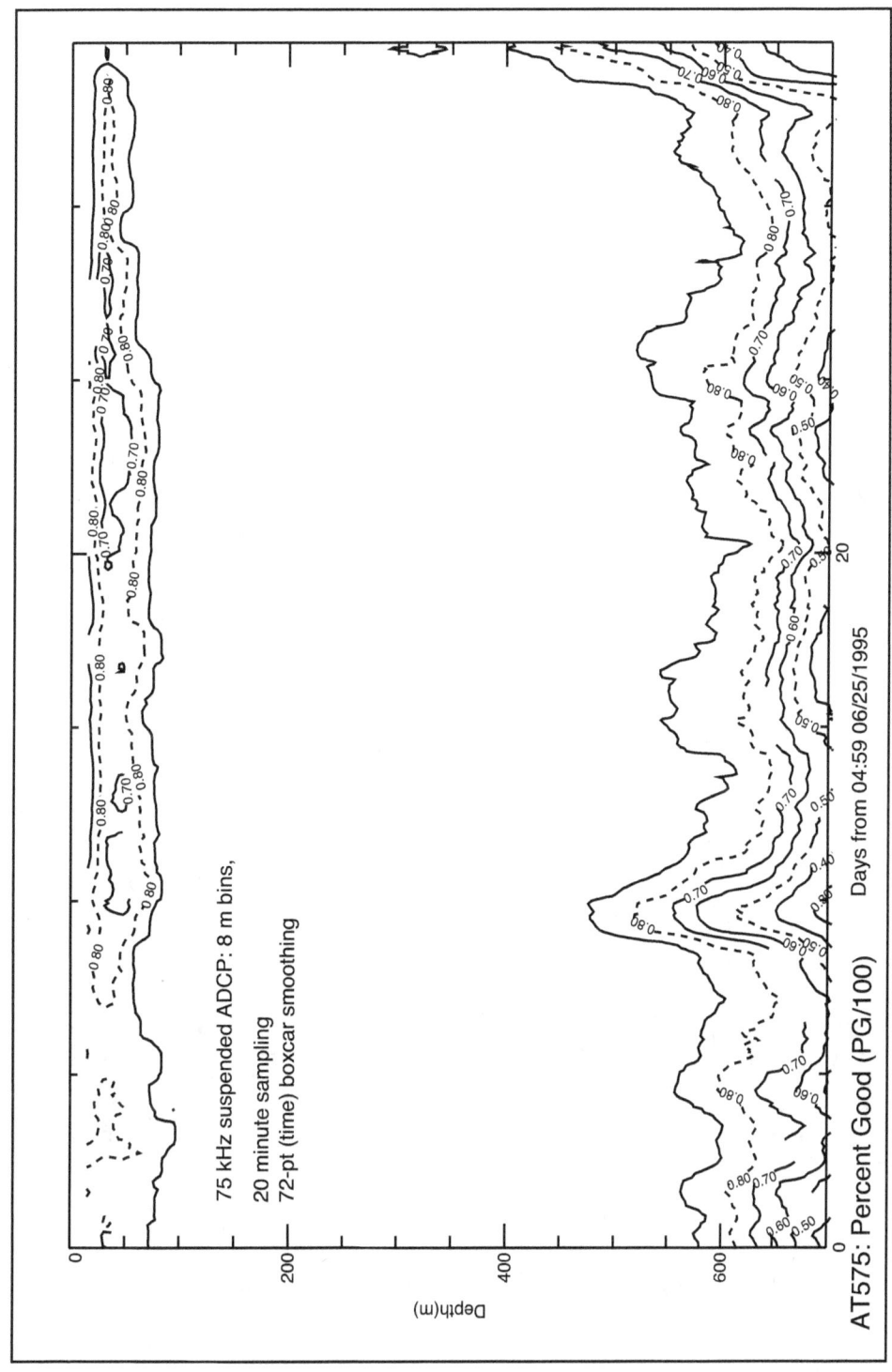

Figure 3.1.3-3. Contours of percentage of good pings per sampling ensemble versus depth and time at same location as Figure 3.1.3-1. Contour interval is 0.10. Data courtesy BP.

21

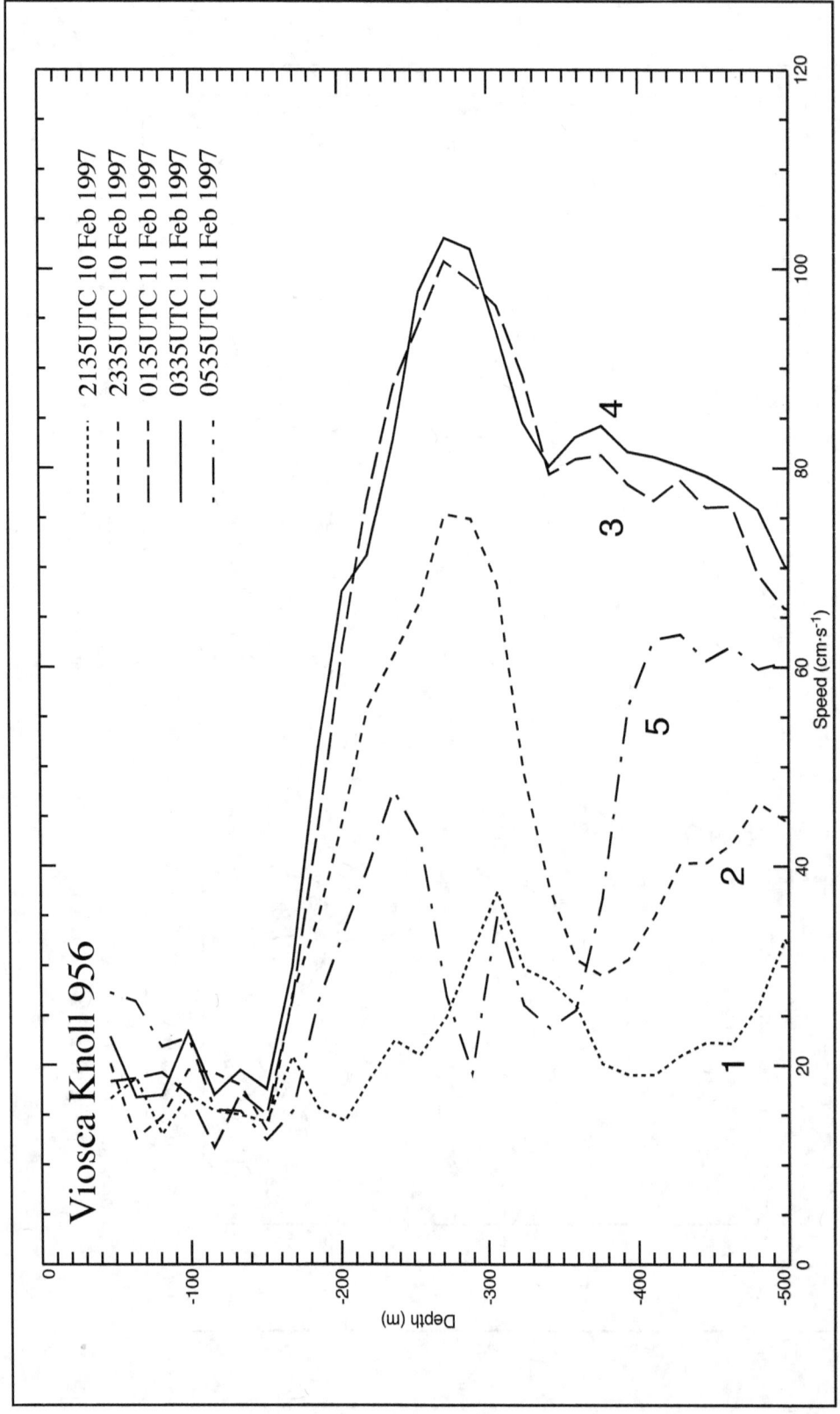

Figure 3.1.4-1. Current profiles made from ADCP two hours apart during the period 2135UTC 10 February 1997 to 0535UTC 11 February 1997 (VK956 case). Data courtesy of Shell Oil Company.

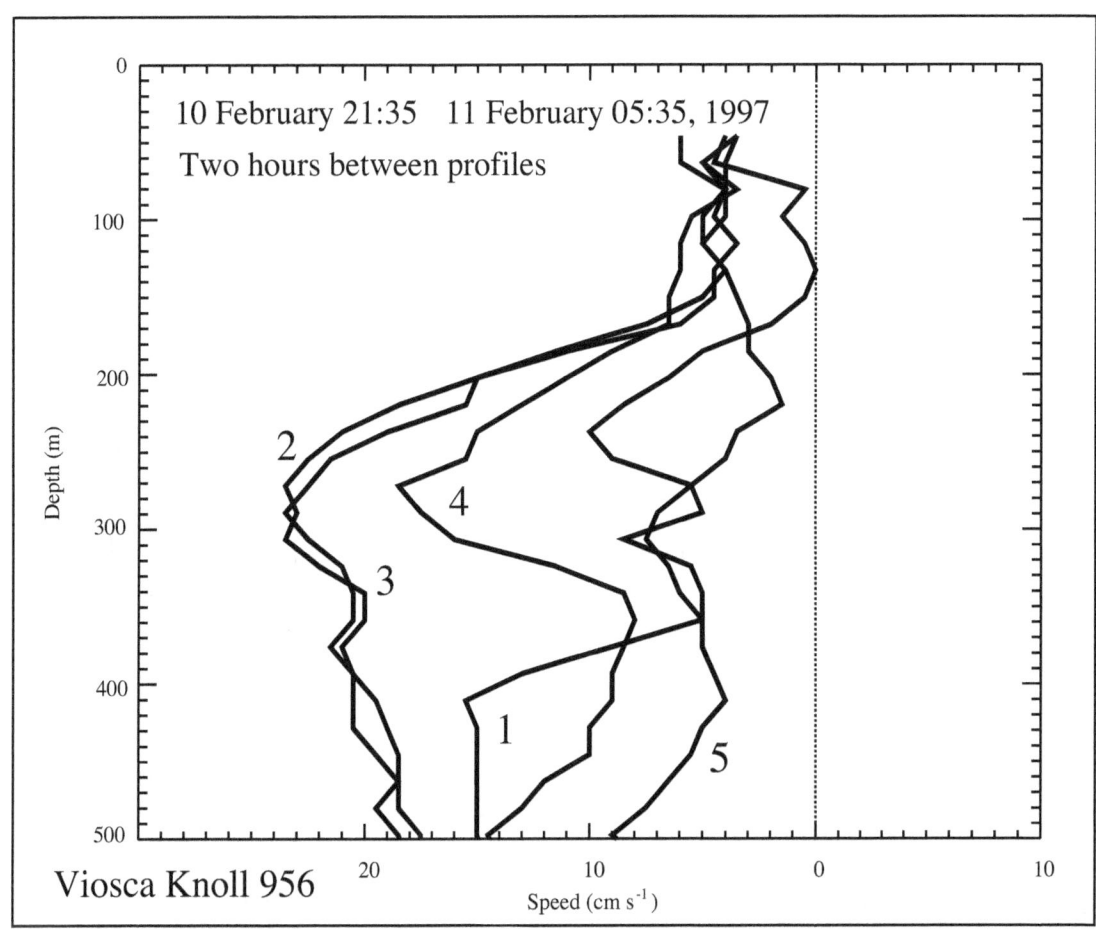

Figure 3.1.4-2. Profiles of vertical velocity (cm·s [1]) made two hours apart during 2135 UTC 10 February 1997 to 0535 UTC 11 February 1997 (VK956 case). Data are courtesy Shell Oil Company. Error velocity is not available during this deployment. Negative values indicate downward flow.

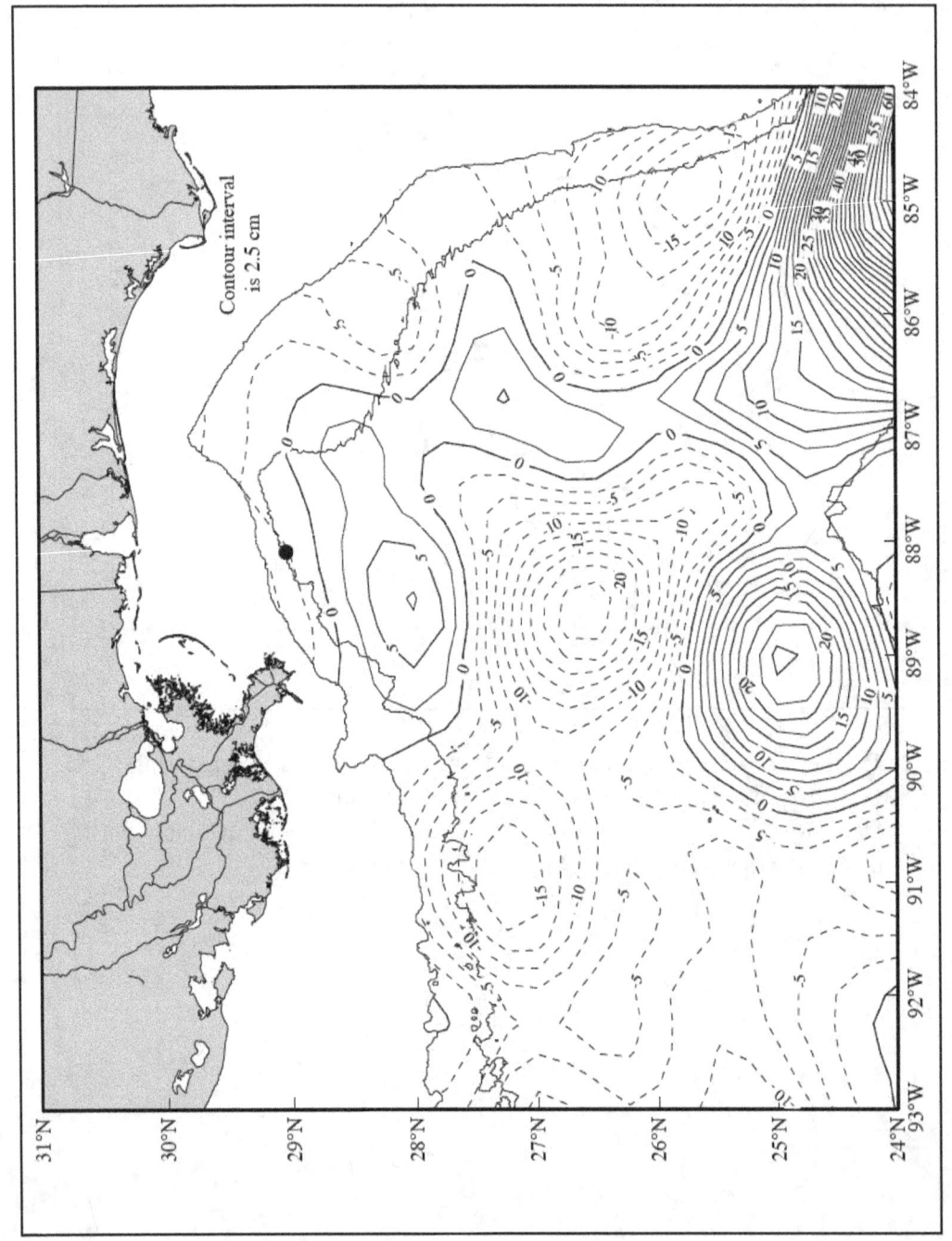

Figure 3.1.4-3. Sea-surface height field from satellite altimeter data for 10 Feb 1997 for VK956 case. The 200 and 1000-m isobath contours are shown. [Data provided by Robert R. Leben, University of Colorado; plot provided courtesy of Ann Jochens, TAMU.

24

south. Eddy Watch charts during this time indicate the presence of a cold core cyclone (Easy Eddy) north of the measurements. Another weak warm core eddy (Eddy Deviant) moved close to the region in late February.

3.1.5   Jet 6 in MC628: 10 April 1997

Figure 3.1.5-1 shows contours of current speed versus depth and time for the jet in MC628 that occurred on 10 April 1997. Data are courtesy of Chevron. The maximum current speeds exceeded 80 cm·s^{-1} at a depth of 300-400 m. Three peaks are observed at different times at the jet's core depth. The main event lasted approximately 24 hours, although currents exceeded 40 cm·s^{-1} for more than 36 hours after the peak current. Currents at 60 m below the surface exceeded 90 cm·s^{-1} 1.5 days before the jet, while currents above 100 m remained greater than 80 cm·s^{-1} much of the time before, during, and after. We also note there was a slight deepening of the speed contours during the period of the jet. The percentage of good pings registered by the ADCP (Figure 3.1.5-2) indicated 100% data return to depth of about 300 m, at which there was a gradual decrease with depth. At 700 m the percent good is relatively constant at 40%. At the depths and times associated with the jet, there was only slight indication of a decrease in percent good. However, estimates of vertical velocity as measured by the ADCP (Figure 3.1.5-3) are correlated with the peaks in horizontal speed maxima. Vertical currents speeds were positive (upward) during the jet and exceeded 5 cm·s^{-1}.

The SSH field (Figure 3.1.5-4) shows that the measurements were made on the western limb of an anticyclonic eddy that was positioned south of the DeSoto Canyon (88°W, 29°N). The eddy was nearly stationary during April-May 1997 and slowly moved westward during June 1997. AVHRR SST imagery (Figure 3.1.5-5) at the time of the jets shows the thermally stratified Gulf of Mexico typical of spring with cooler temperatures to the north and warmer to the south. The warm region between 86°W-87°W and 28°N coincides with a high region of SSH seen in Figure 3.1.5-4.

3.1.6   Jet 7 in GC505: 4 November 1997

A 75-kHz ADCP was deployed from a drill ship for routine ocean monitoring in Green Canyon Lease Block 505 from 7 October 1997 through 15 March 1998. Data are courtesy of Texaco. The total water depth at this location was 1306 m. The ADCP was suspended at 16 m below the sea surface and was set to record at roughly 20-minute intervals and 8-m bins (Figure 3.6-1). Eddy El Dorado detached from the Loop Current in September 1997 and moved westward, first passing south of the instrument. A cyclonic feature appeared to be over the deployment location during early November (Figure 3.1.6-2). Beginning on 4 November, a subsurface oscillation event with amplitudes greater than 40 cm·s^{-1} was seen between 150 and 350 m depth. These oscillations had a period of 24 hours. The event lasted nine days, although the period that the speeds exceed 30 cm·s^{-1} was only on the order of a few hours. A speed minimum was seen between 50 and 150 m; there was no indication of significant diurnal variability in the near-surface (0-50 m) layers. We note that current speeds between 300 and 500 m persistently exceeded 20 cm·s^{-1} during the 24-hr oscillations. The percentage good data quality indicator shows a decrease of 20-30% during the peak speeds of the oscillation (Figure 3.1.6-3).

25

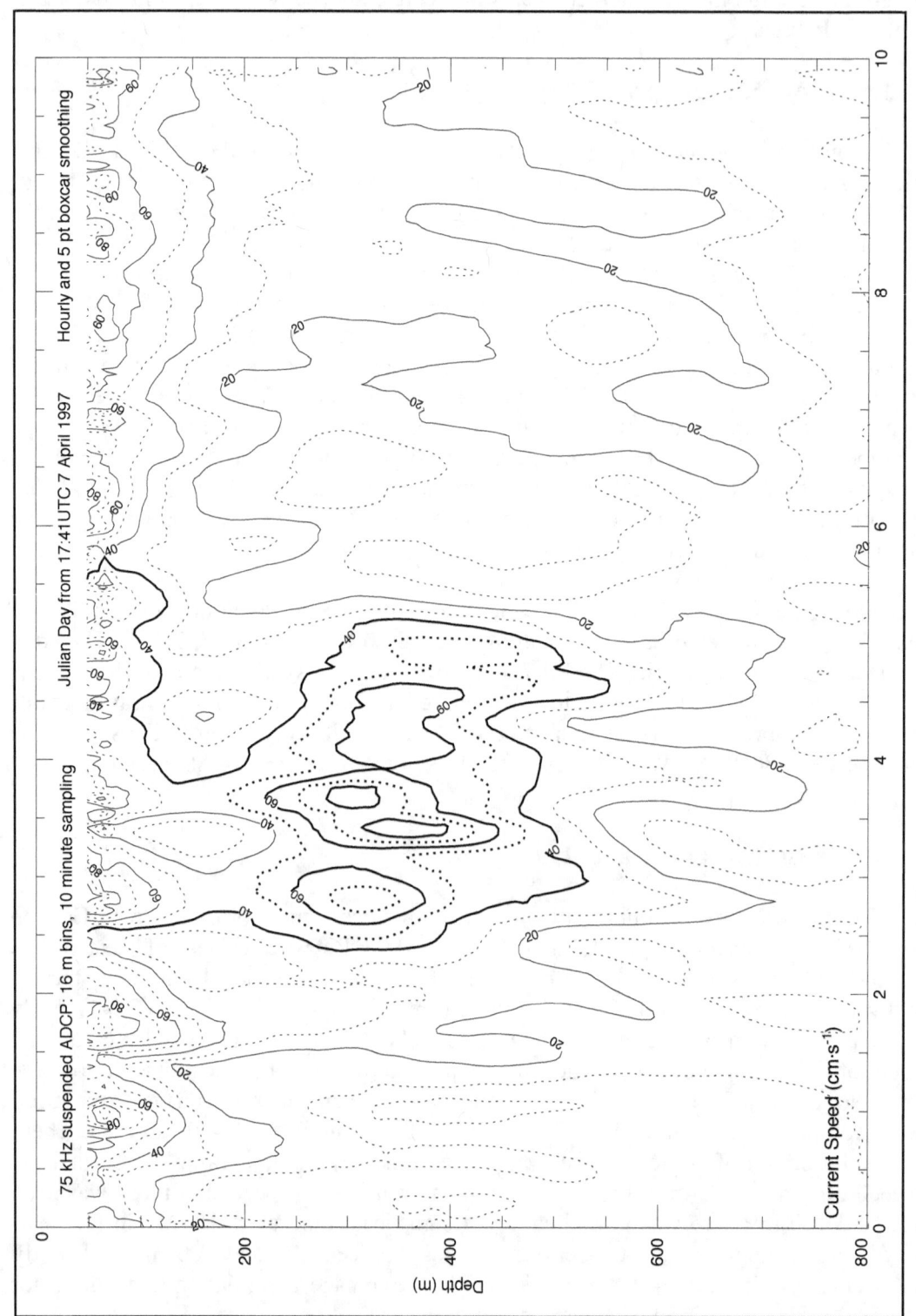

Figure 3.1.5-1. Contours of current speed versus depth and time showing subsurface jet occurring in lease block MC628. Contour interval is 10 cm·s⁻¹; data are in 16-m bins and 10-minute sampling interval. Data courtesy Chevron.

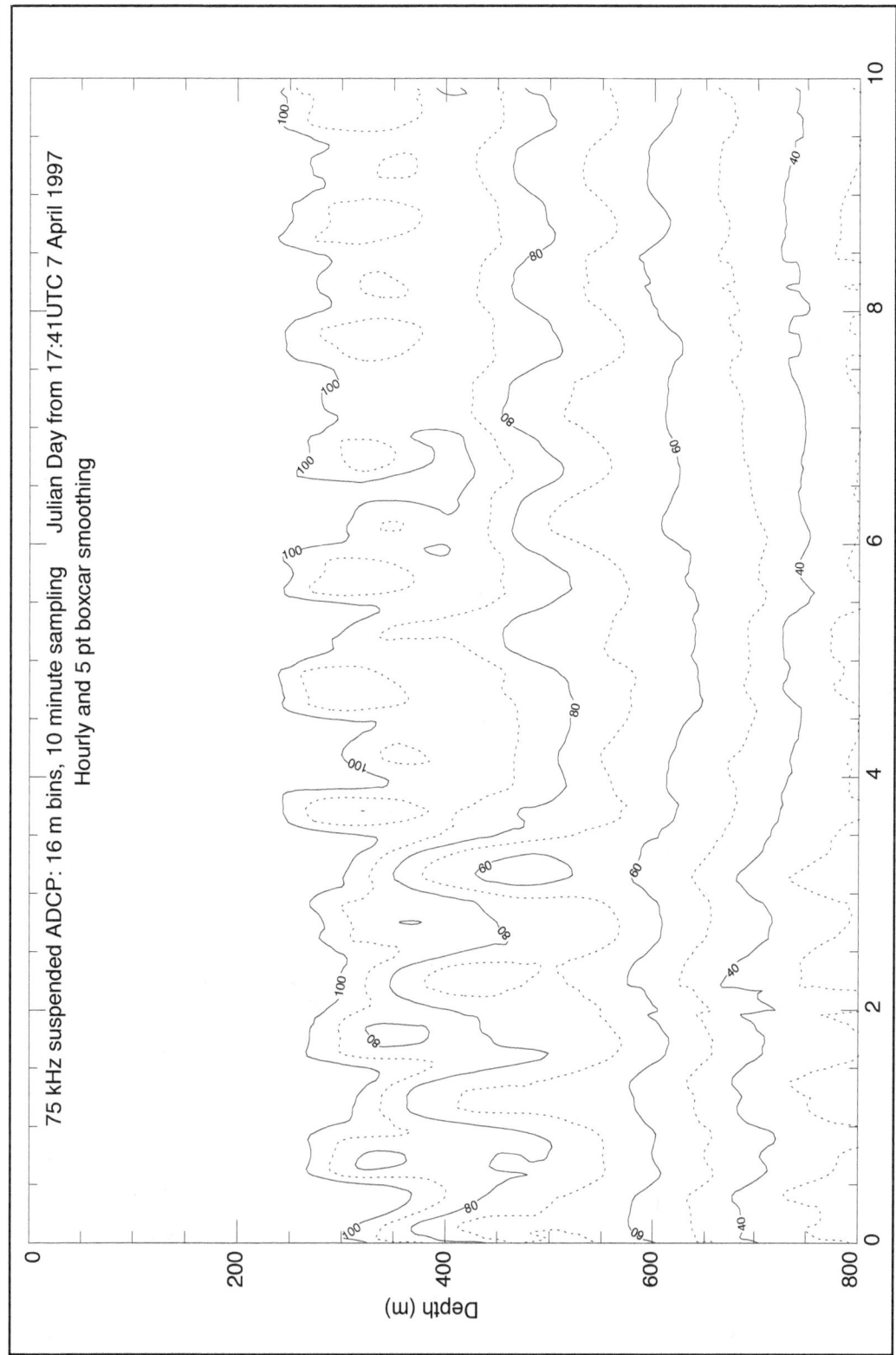

Figure 3.1.5-2. Contours of percentage of good pings per sampling ensemble versus depth at same time and location as Figure 3.1.5-1 (MC 628). Contour interval is 10%. Data courtesy Chevron.

27

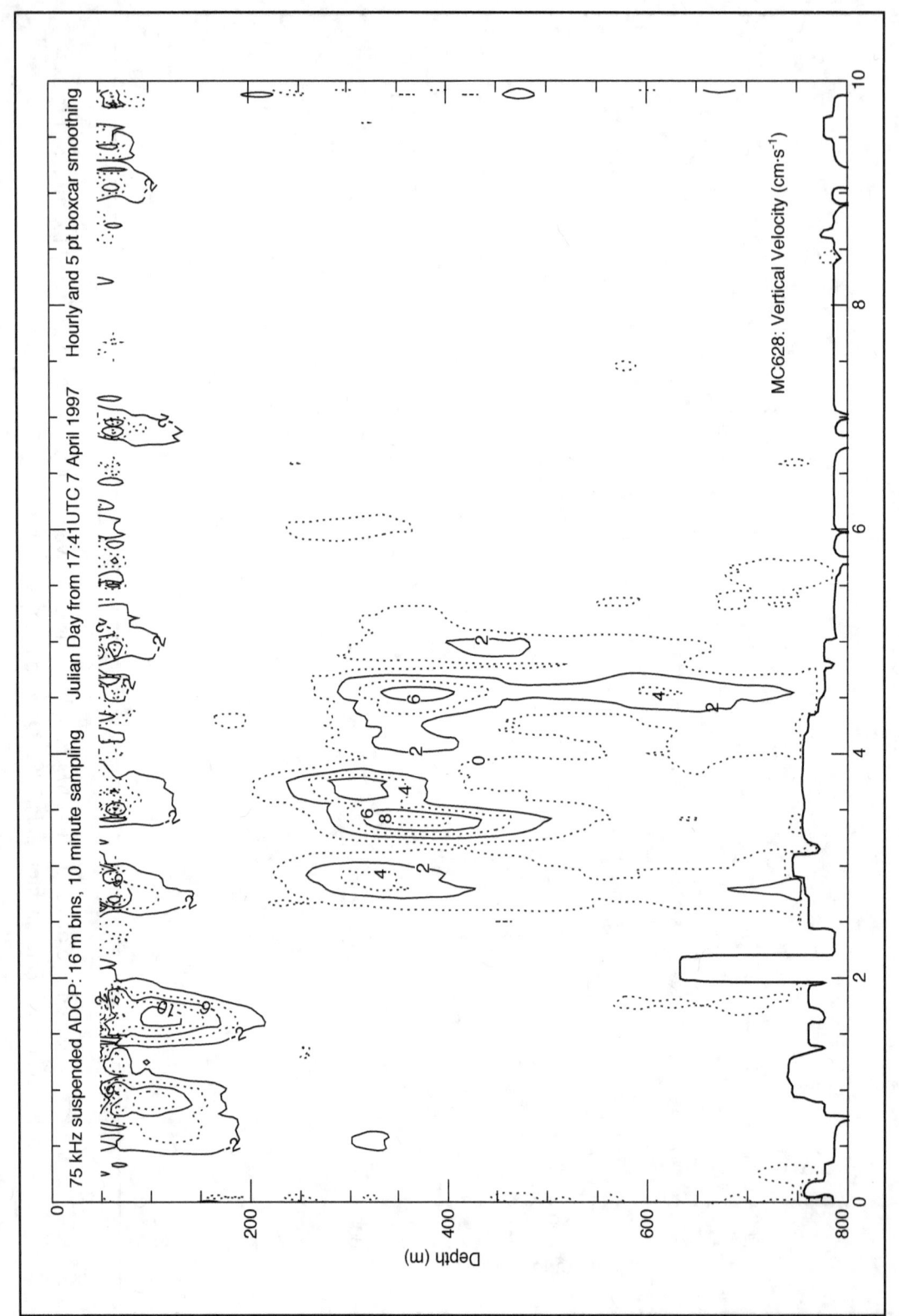

Figure 3.1.5-3. Contours of vertical velocity (cm·s⁻¹) versus depth and time at same time and location as Figure 3.1.5-1 (MC 628). Contour interval is 1 cm·s⁻¹. Data courtesy Chevron.

28

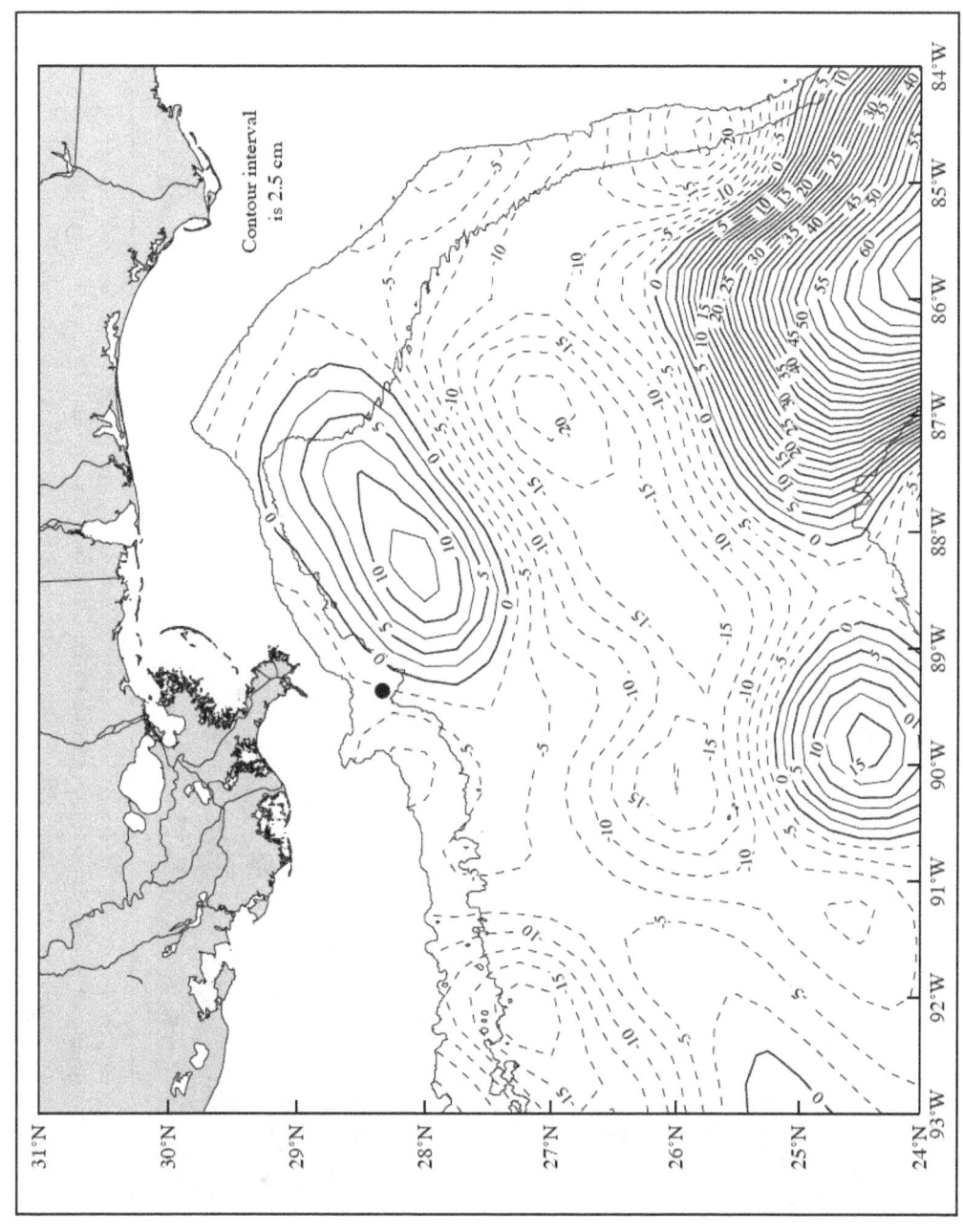

Figure 3.1.5-4. Sea-surface height field from satellite altimeter data for 10 April 1997 for MC628 jet (dot). The 200 and 1000-m isobath contours are shown. The filled circle shows the jet location. [Data provided by Robert R. Leben, University of Colorado, Plot provided courtesy of Ann Jochens, TAMU.]

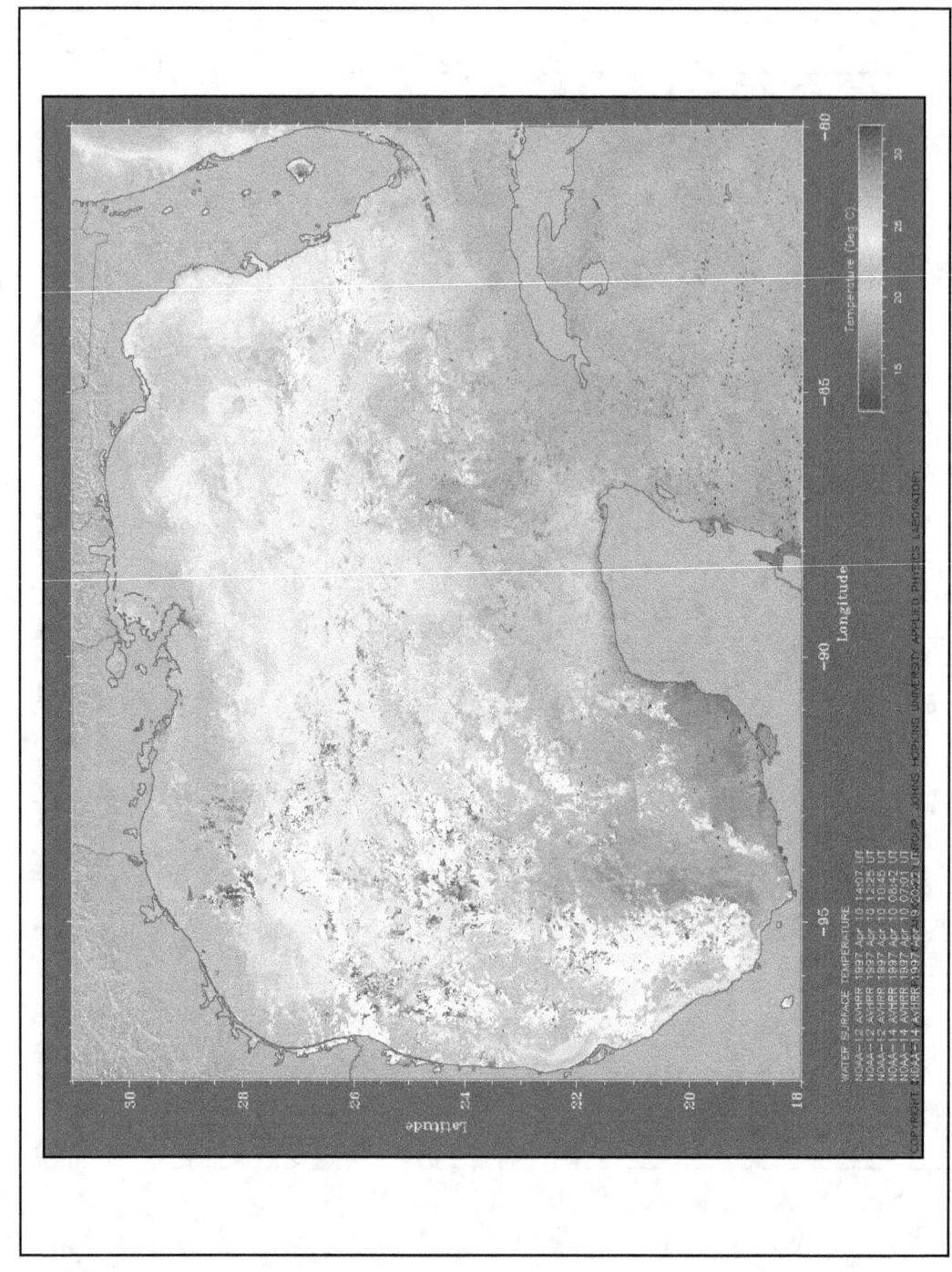

Figure 3.1.5-5. AVHRR image of sea-surface temperature of the Gulf of Mexico on 10 Apr 1997. Image is an average of 7 images averaged over a 2-day period. Data courtesy of Johns Hopkins Applied Physical Laboratory.

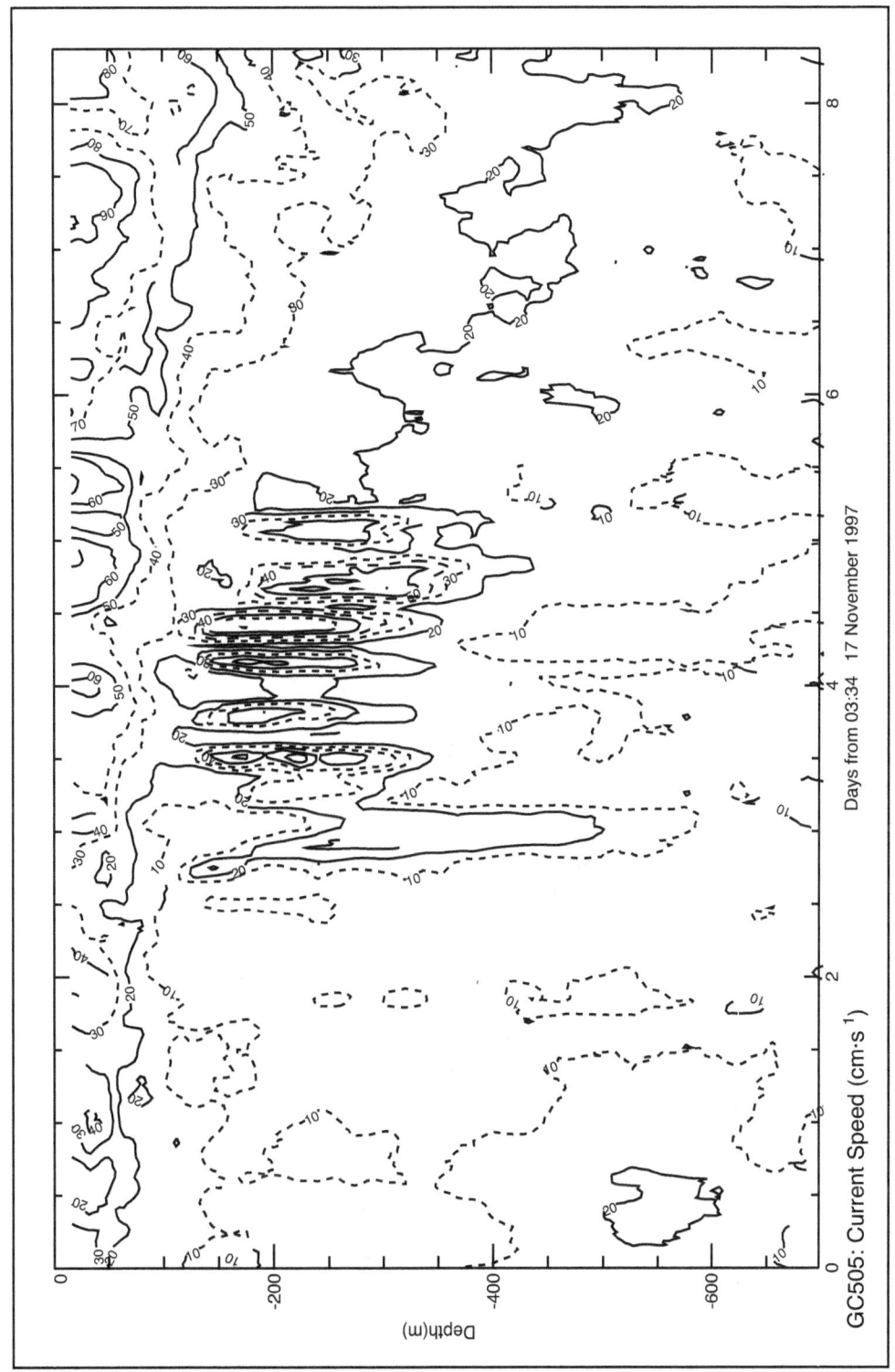

Figure 3.1.6-1. Contours of current speed versus depth and time showing subsurface jet occurring in lease block GC505 during 4 November 1997. Contour interval is 10 cm·s⁻¹; data are in 8 m bins and 19-minute sampling. Data are courtesy of Texaco.

31

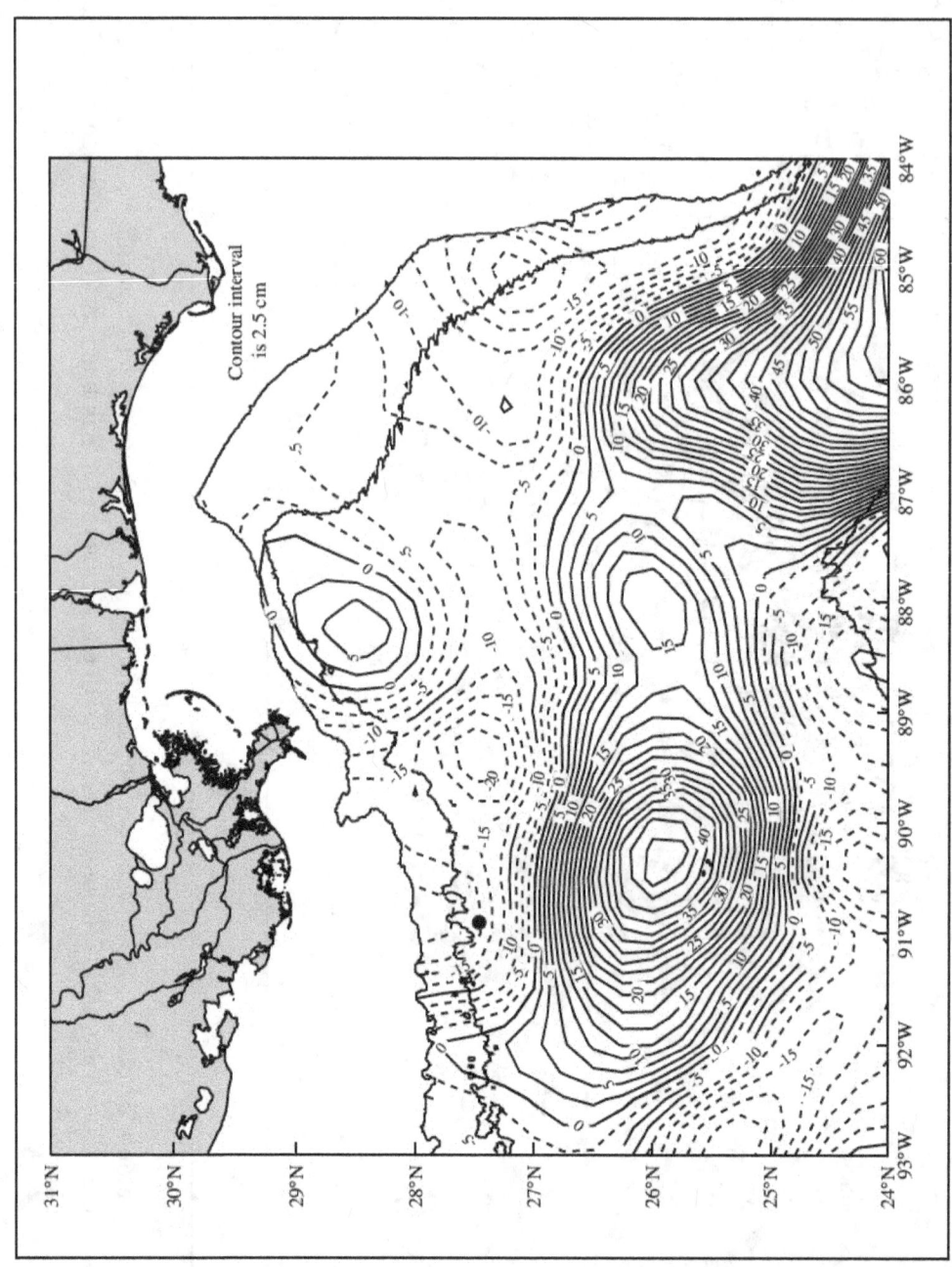

Figure 3.1.6-2. Sea-surface height field from satellite altimeter data for 9 November 1997 for GC505 long case. The 200 and 1000-m isobath contours are shown. [Data provided by Robert R. Leben, University of Colorado; plot courtesy of Ann Jochens]

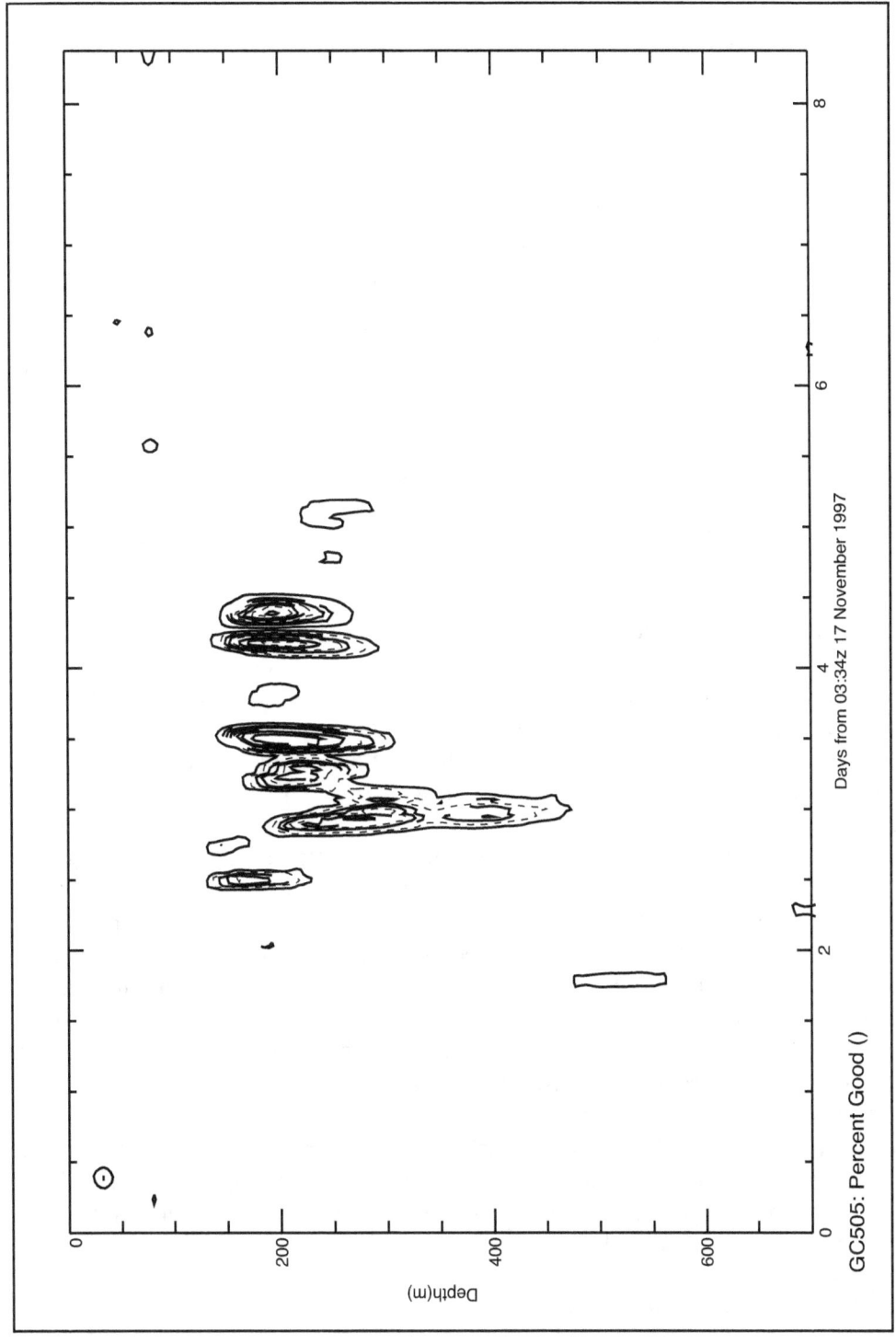

Figure 3.1.6-3. Contours of percentage of good pings per sampling ensemble versus depth at the same time and locations as Figure 3.1.6-1 (GC505). Contour interval is 10%. Data are courtesy of Texaco.

33

3.1.7   Jet 8 in GC505: 20 November 1997

Roughly one week after the jet event described in Section 3.1.6, a second jet event occurred in GC505. During the middle and end of November 1997, Eddy El Dorado pushed north over the deployment location with currents exceeding 80 cm·s^{-1}. As the leading edge of the eddy passed by the instrument on 20 November, another packet of current oscillations occurred between 150 and 350 m depth (Figure 3.1.7-1). These oscillations appear to be a series of short-lived current pulses lasting on the order of 4-8 hours. As before, there was no indication of such oscillations above 150 m. The percent good decreased sharply during the peak speeds indicating a dramatic reduction in data quality during this event (Figure 3.1.7-2).

The reduction of data quality during these two events at GC505 casts serious doubt on the validity of these data. Since the depth of the jet is the same for both events, it may be that the drill string or other structure was interfering with the acoustic beams during these measurements. Vertical and error velocity as well as beam correlation and echo intensity were not available to us for analysis.

3.1.8   Jet 9 in GC236: 9 April 1998

The data containing this jet was provided by Marathon Oil Company for use in the MMS Deepwater Reanalysis Program. The jet was located in lease block GC236 (27.7302°N, 91.1419°W). Peak current speeds exceeded 62 cm·s^{-1} at 180 m depth and the event lasted on the order of 4 hours. A contour plot of current speed versus depth and time is shown in Figure 3.1.8-1 (upper). Also plotted are contours of vertical velocity versus depth and time. Vertical and error velocities reached -10 and -12.5 cm·s^{-1} during the peak horizontal current speeds (Figure 3.1.8-1 lower). Such large vertical and error velocities are indicative of possible inhomogeneous flow fields. As described in Section 3.2, standard acoustic current profilers were not designed to accurately reconstruct horizontal flow fields in the presence of substantial inhomogeneous flow fields. In addition, echo intensities of one of the instrument's acoustic beams show an appreciable dip during the event indicating that rig interference may also be at play here. Contributing to the uncertainty in the quality of this record is that the instrument was turned off for several days after the measurements shown in Figure 3.1.8-1. Then the instrument was intermittently turned on and off for several more days. Therefore, we surmise that rig operations may have affected the data collection during this time. There is no record that rig operations were affected by subsurface currents. The SSH field (Figure 3.1.8-2) shows Eddy Fourchon centered at 88.5°W, 25°N. A filament extended north almost to the measurement location. The eddy's presence is confirmed in SST imagery (Figure 3.1.8-3), where the northern front of the eddy shows several long wavelength oscillations running along the shelf edge. A tongue of cool shelf water was seen being advected off the shelf and into deep water on the eastern side of the eddy, southwest of the Mississippi River delta.

3.1.9   Jet 10 in DC977: 28 September 1998

An interesting phenomenon resembling a subsurface jet has been identified in the MMS Eddy Intrusion Study data. On September 27, 1998, Hurricane Georges moved over the DeSoto

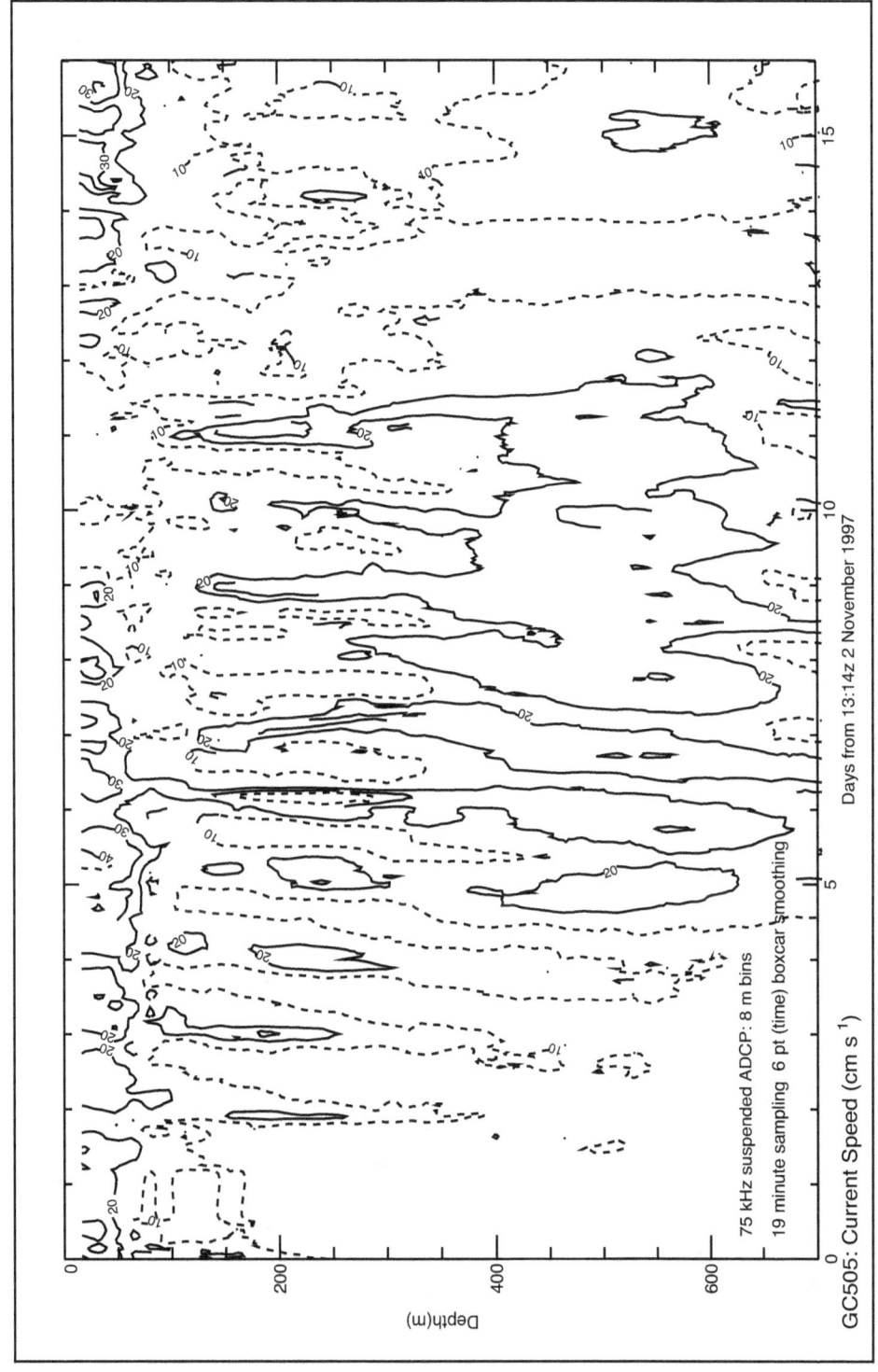

Figure 3.1.7-1. Contours of current speed versus depth and time showing subsurface jet oscillations occurring in lease block GC505 on 20 November 1997. Contour interval is 10 cm s[-1]; data are in 8-m bins and 19-minute sampling. Data are courtesy Texaco.

35

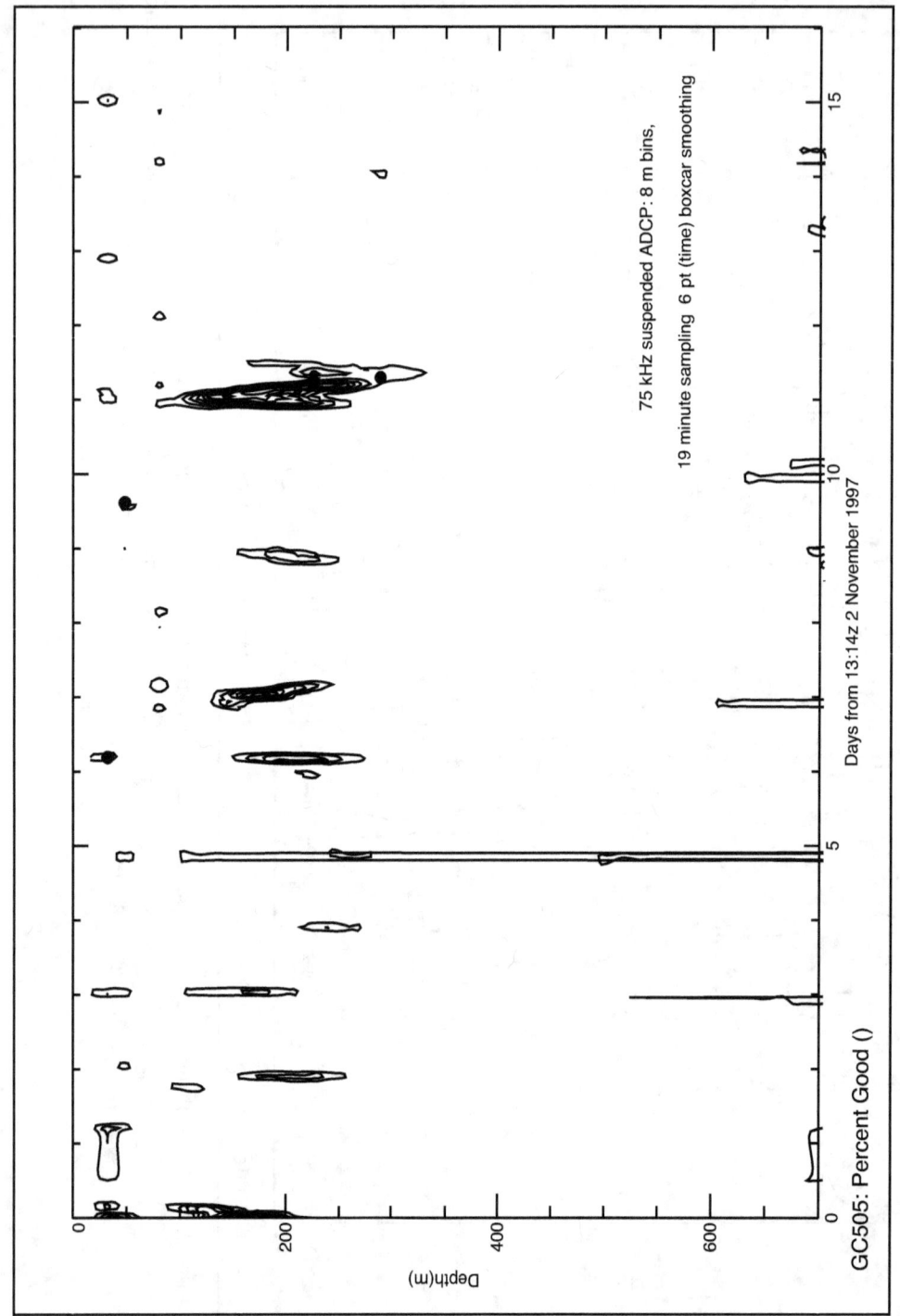

Figure 3.1.7-2. Contours of percentage of good pings per sampling interval versus depth and time at same location as Figure 3.1.7-1. Contour interval is 10%. Data are courtesy Texaco.

36

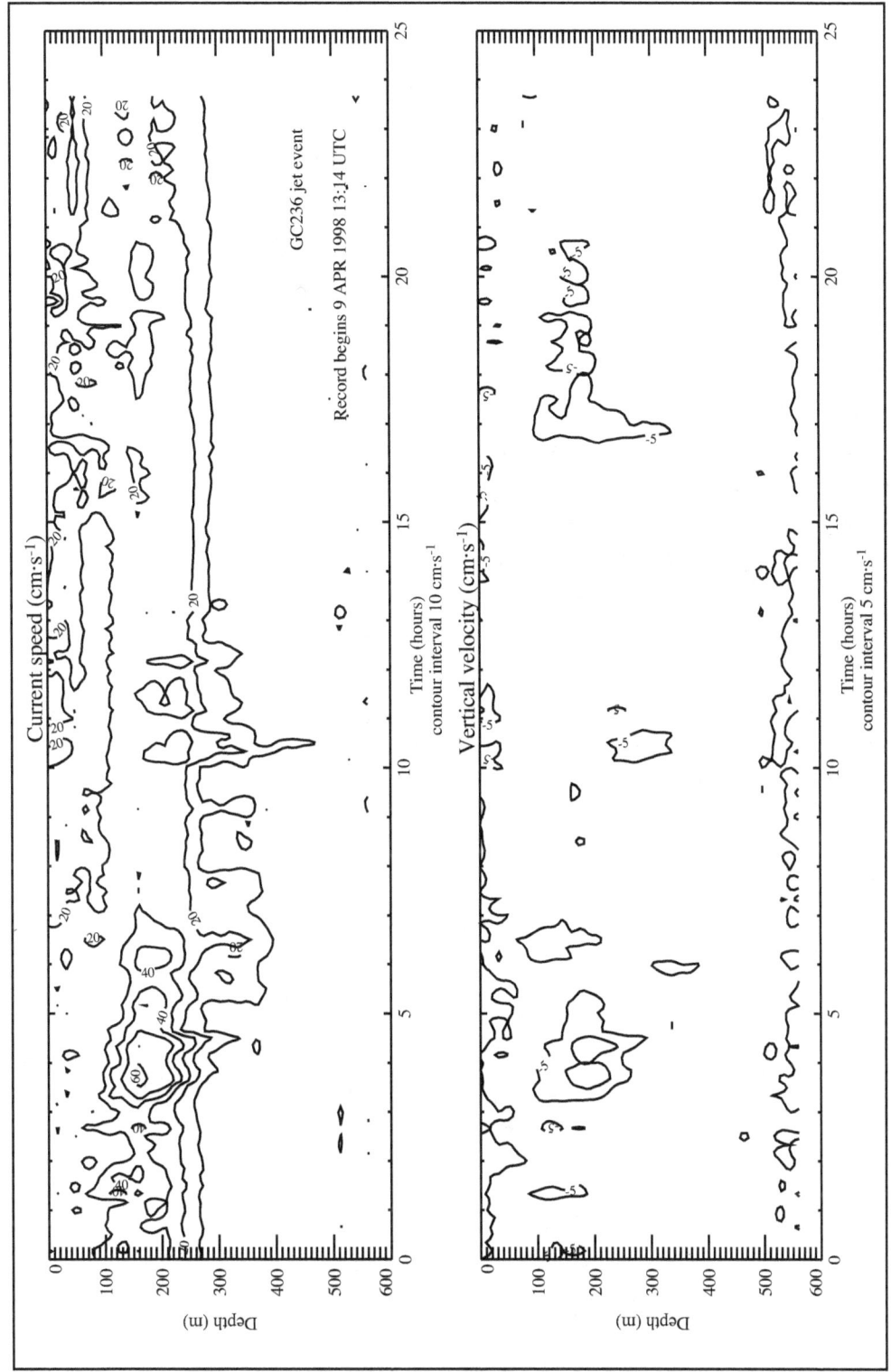

Figure 3.1.8-1. (Top) Contours of current speed versus depth and time showing subsurface jet occurring in lease block GC236. Contour interval is 10 cm·s⁻¹. (Bottom) Contours of vertical velocity versus depth and time. Contour interval is 5 cm·s⁻¹. Data are in 8-m bins and 20-minute sampling interval. Data are courtesy of Marathon. Note: time scales in both plots are hours.

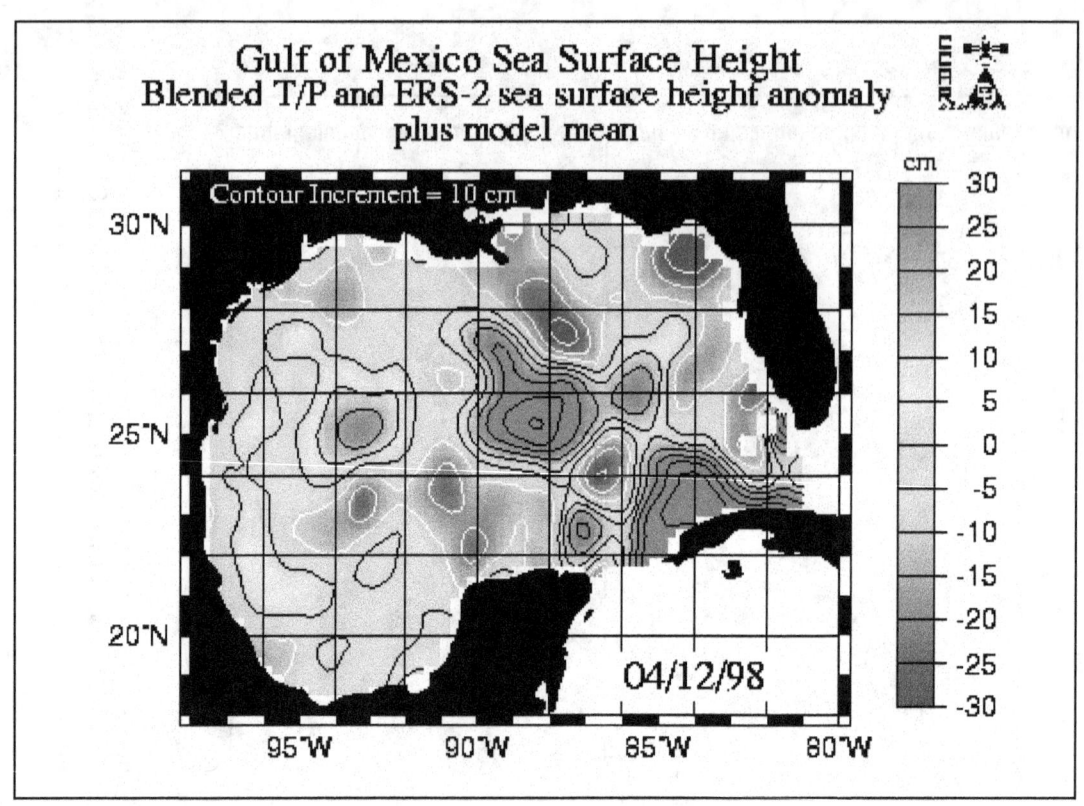

Figure 3.1.8-2. Sea-surface height (anomaly plus model mean) of the Gulf of Mexico based on blended TOPEX/Poseidon and ERS-2 satellite altimeter on 12 April 1998 during GC236 jet event. Coutour interval is 10 cm. Image courtesy Dr. Robert Leben (University of Colorado).

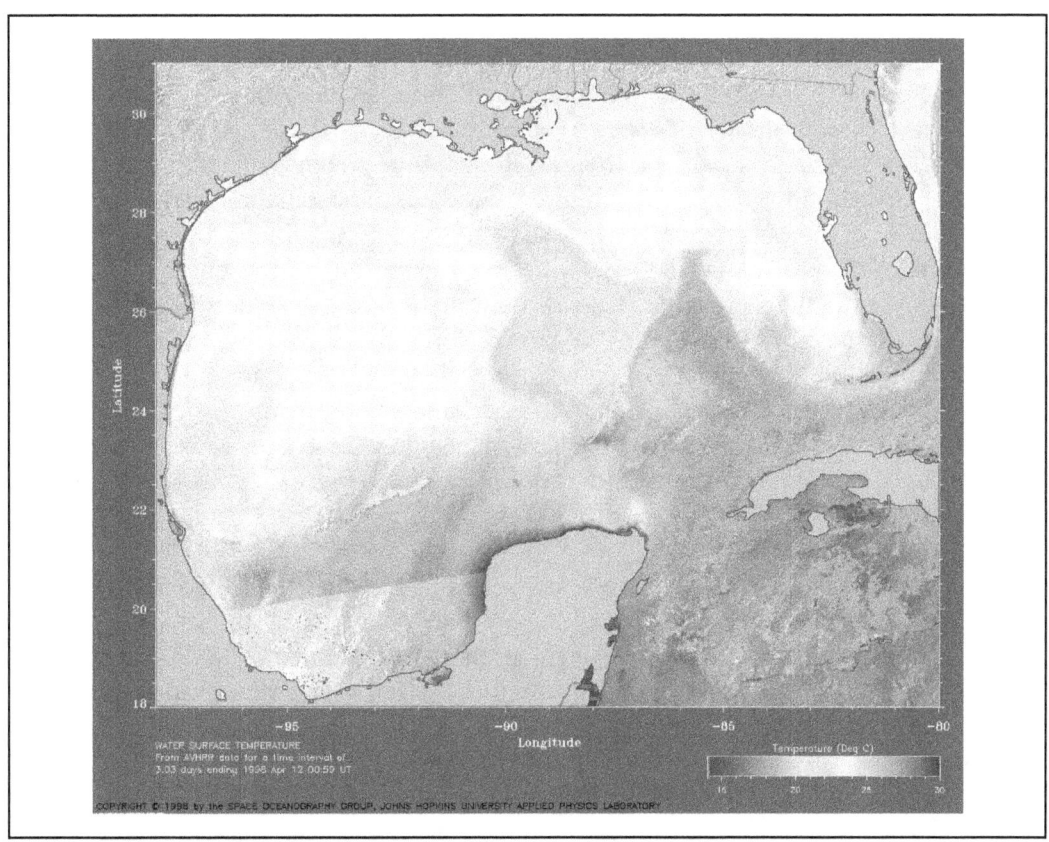

Figure 3.1.8-3. AVHRR image of sea-surface temperature of the Gulf of Mexico on 12 April 1998 during GC236 jet event. Image is average of 3.03 days. Image is courtesy of Johns Hopkins Applied Physics Laboratory.

Canyon Region in the northeastern Gulf of Mexico producing strong near-surface currents in excess of 150 cm·s^{-1}. As the storm passed and made landfall, the near-surface currents over the continental slope and rise oscillated for several days at the local inertial period. Figure 3.1.9-1 shows the 18-50 hour band-pass filtered component current speeds during September-October 1998. At 12 m, the filtered current speeds were greater than 60 cm·s^{-1} (150 cm·s^{-1} unfiltered) during the time of the storm's passing, then oscillated with gradually decreasing amplitude for about 10 days. Deeper in the water column (72 m), the inertial oscillations began about the time of the hurricane's passing and gradually increased to a peak magnitude of about 40 cm·s^{-1} one week after the storm passed. At 500 m, a packet of inertial period energy is clearly seen beginning 10 days after the storm first affected the near surface and lasting roughly 10 days with peak speeds of about 25 cm·s^{-1}. Figure 3.1.9-1 clearly shows the downward propagation of inertial band energy after the passage of an intense cyclone. We emphasize that the inertial wave packet seen at 500 m was likely generated at a location remote from this mooring. Based on these observations, it is likely that some subsurface jets could be caused by the vertical propagation and horizontal migration of inertial energy days or weeks after a significant atmospheric event.

SSH altimeter data (Figure 3.1.9-2) show a fairly strong cyclone (minimum SSH less than -20 cm) centered approximately 80 km south of the mooring at the time of the jet. The Loop Current was south of 26°N during the months of September though November 1998. AVHRR sea surface temperature imagery shows considerable cooling of the sea surface due to the passage of the hurricane (Figure 3.1.9-3).

3.1.10 Jet 11 in GC506: 25 October 1998

A 75-kHz ADCP was deployed from a drill ship for routine ocean monitoring in Green Canyon Lease Block 506 from 6 September 1998 until 14 November 1998. The instrument was set to sample at 20-minute intervals and 8 m bins. The data were provided courtesy of Chevron/Texaco. No Loop Current Eddies were in the vicinity of this location during the deployment. Eddy Fourchon had moved into the western Gulf during August 1998. The Loop Current was retracted south of 26°N. A weak cyclone was due west of the instrument and a larger more intense cyclone was located east and southeast as seen in the SSH field of 25 October 1998 (Figure 3.1.10-1). A subsurface jet is seen in the current record beginning on 25 October and lasting about 3 days (Figure 3.1.10-2). The velocity core was between 200- and 400-m depth with peak speeds exceeding 80 cm·s^{-1}. The percent good field during this jet was particularly bad showing reductions to less than 20% (Figure 3.1.10-3). The reduced percent good extends to the range well below the depth of the jet. Thus, the data quality during this particular event must be viewed as suspect.

3.1.11 Jet 12 in EW913: 16 August 1999

A series of 19 screen images of ADCP speed/direction profiles measured by Burlington Industries on 15-18 August 1999, show the development of the jet in lease block EW913. The images chronicle the development of a subsurface jet, which reached a maximum speed of

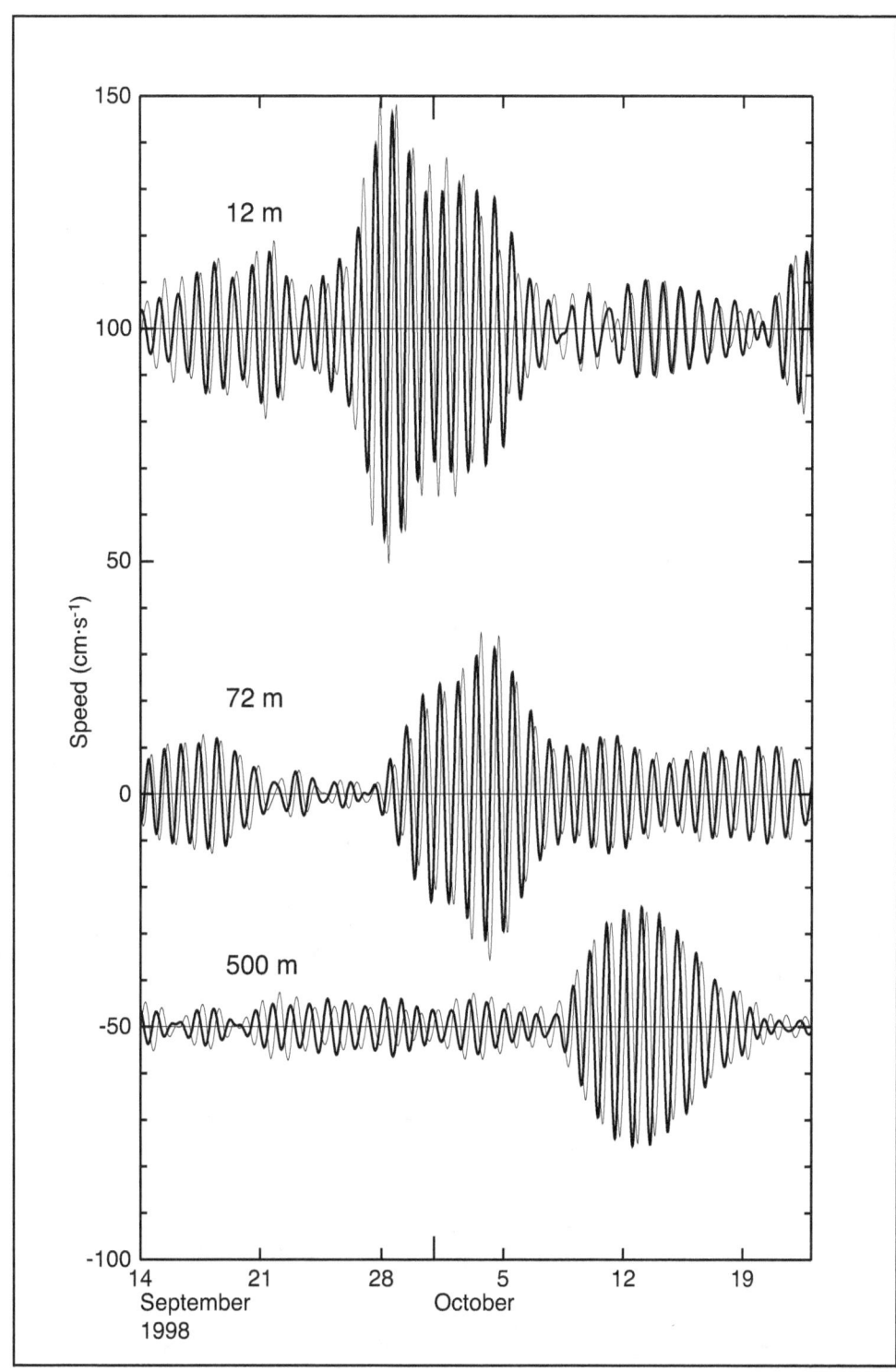

Figure 3.1.9-1. Current components from 18-29 hr band-passed records from mooring C3 in MMS-sponsored DeSoto Canyon Eddy Intrusion Study located in 1,300-m water depth. Hurricane Georges passed over the region on 27 Sept 1998. Heavy line is east/west component; light line is north/south component.

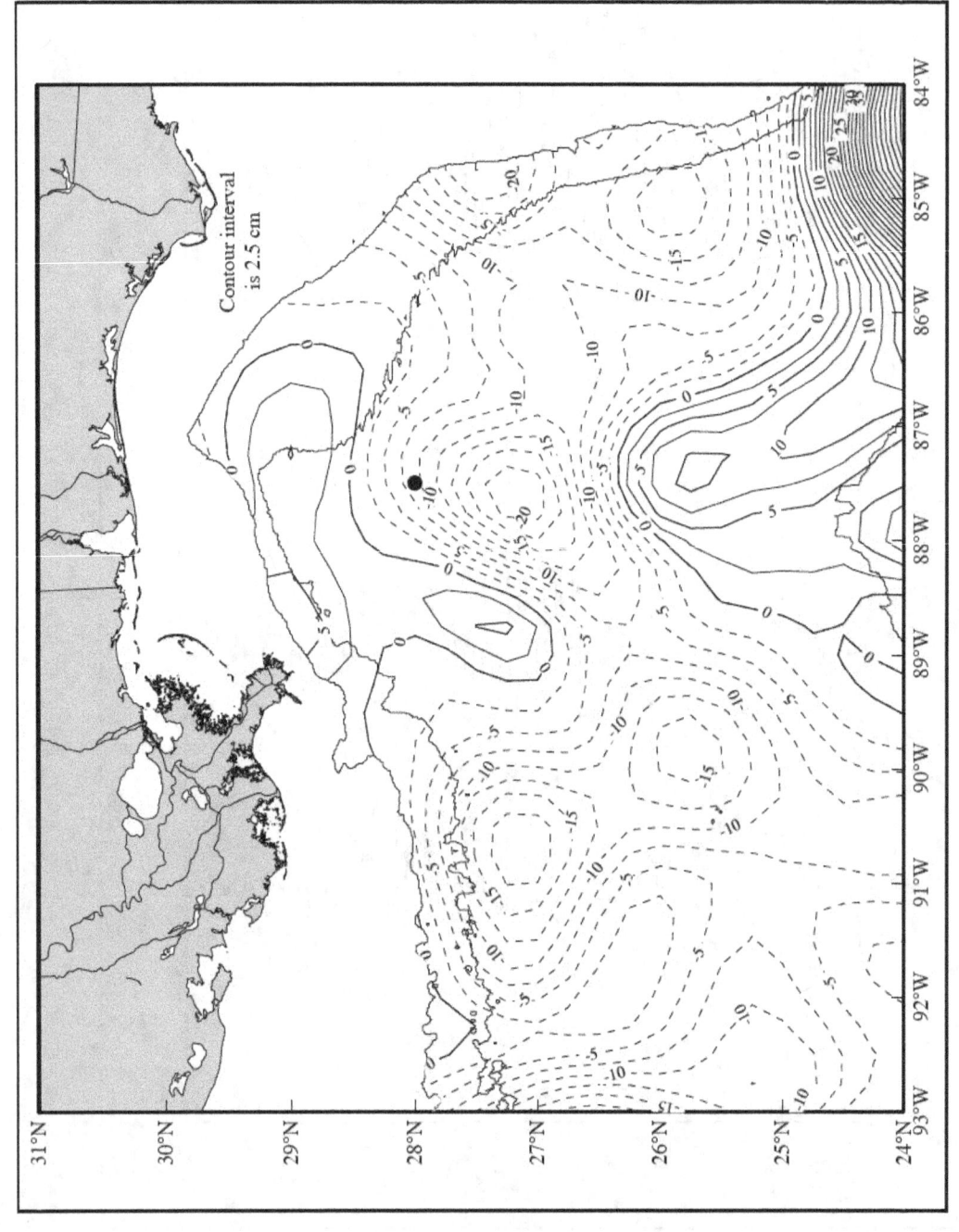

Figure 3.1.9-2. Sea-surface height field from satellite altimeter data for 28 Sept 1998 for DC977 case. The 200 and 1000-m isobath contours are shown. [Data provided by Robert R. Leben, University of Colorado; plot provided courtesy of Ann Jochens, TAMU.]

42

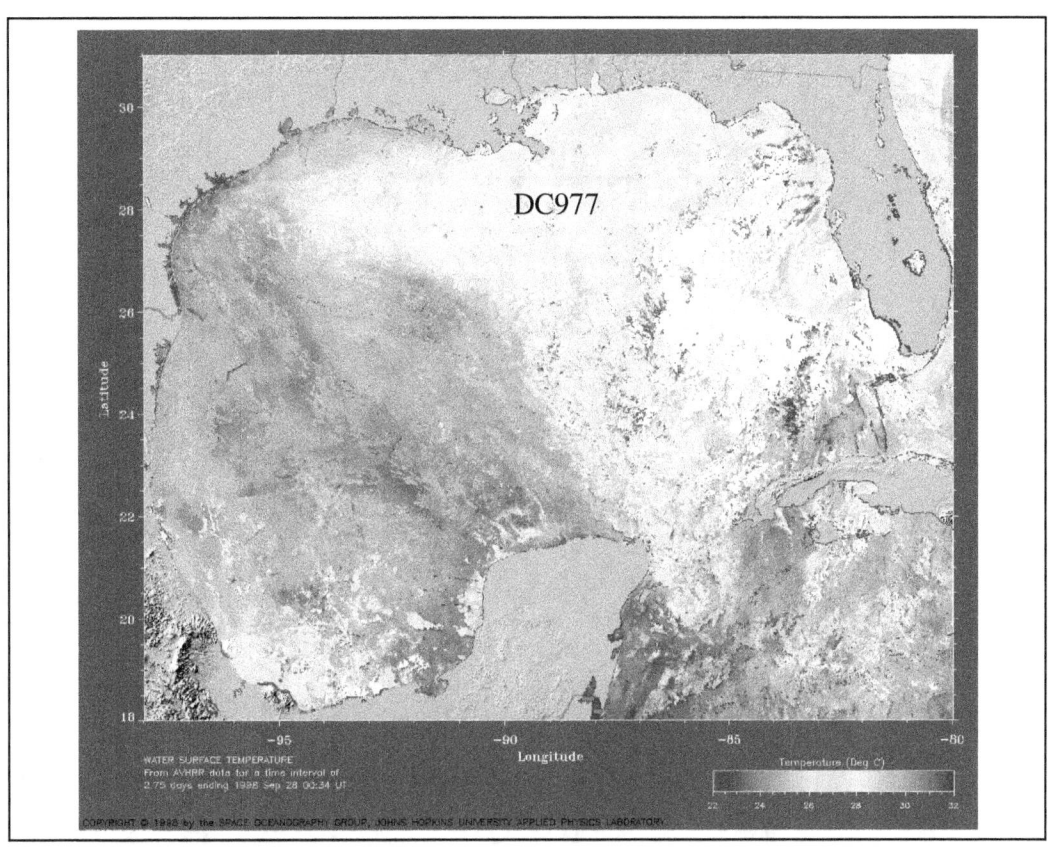

Figure 3.1.9-3. AVHRR image of sea-surface temperature of the Gulf of Mexico on 28 September 1998. Image is an average over a 2.75-day period. Image is courtesy of Johns Hopkins Applied Physics Laboratory.

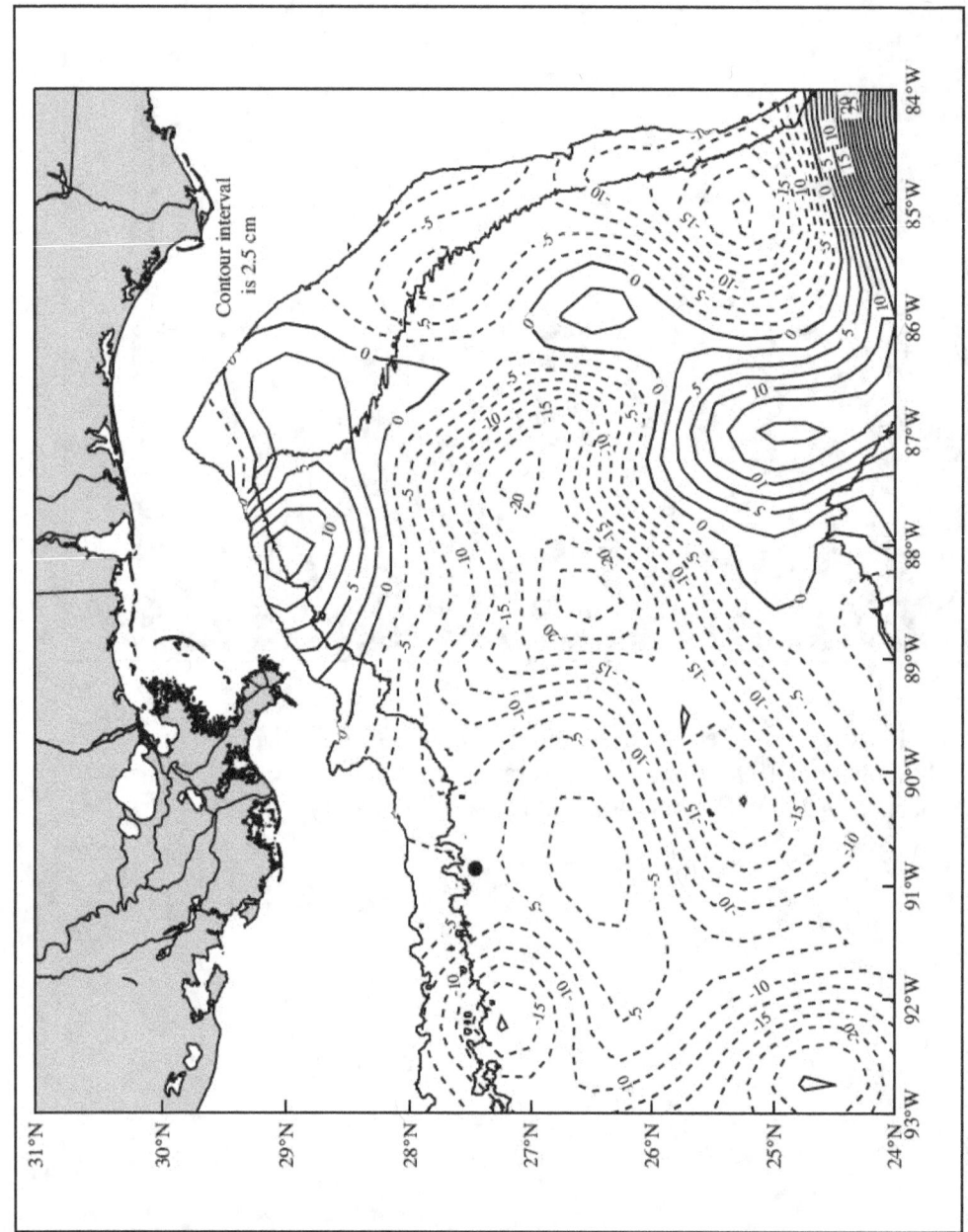

Figure 3.1.10-1. Sea-surface height field from satellite altimeter data for 25 October 1998 for GC506 case (dot). The 200 and 1000-m isobath contours are shown. [Data provided by Robert R. Leben, University of Colorado; plot is courtesy of Ann Jochens (TAMU)]

44

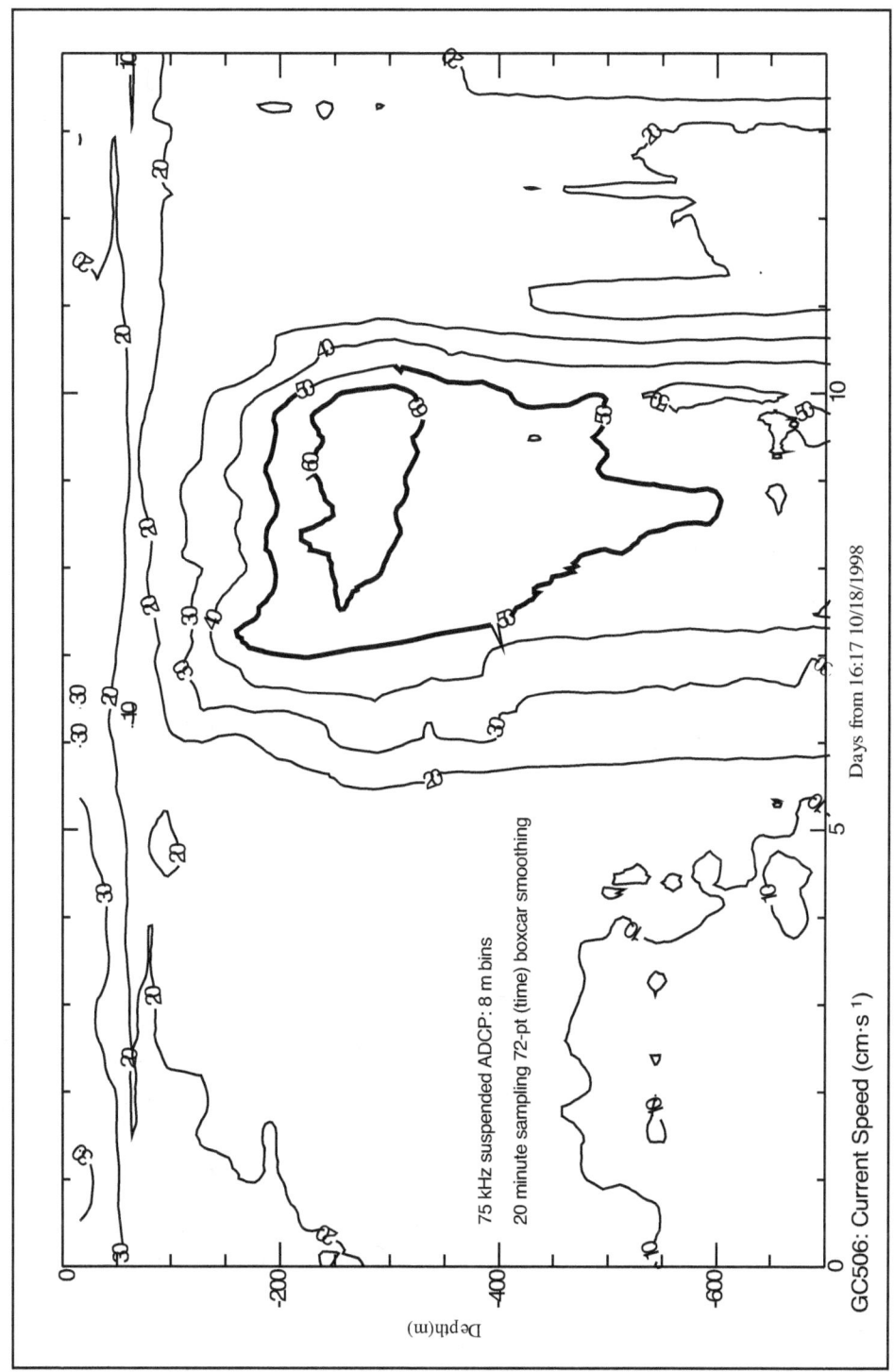

Figure 3.1.10-2. Contours of current speed versus depth and time showing subsurface jet in lease block GC506. Contour interval is 10 cm·s⁻¹; data are in 8-m bins and 20-minute sampling interval. Data are courtesy of Texaco/Chevron.

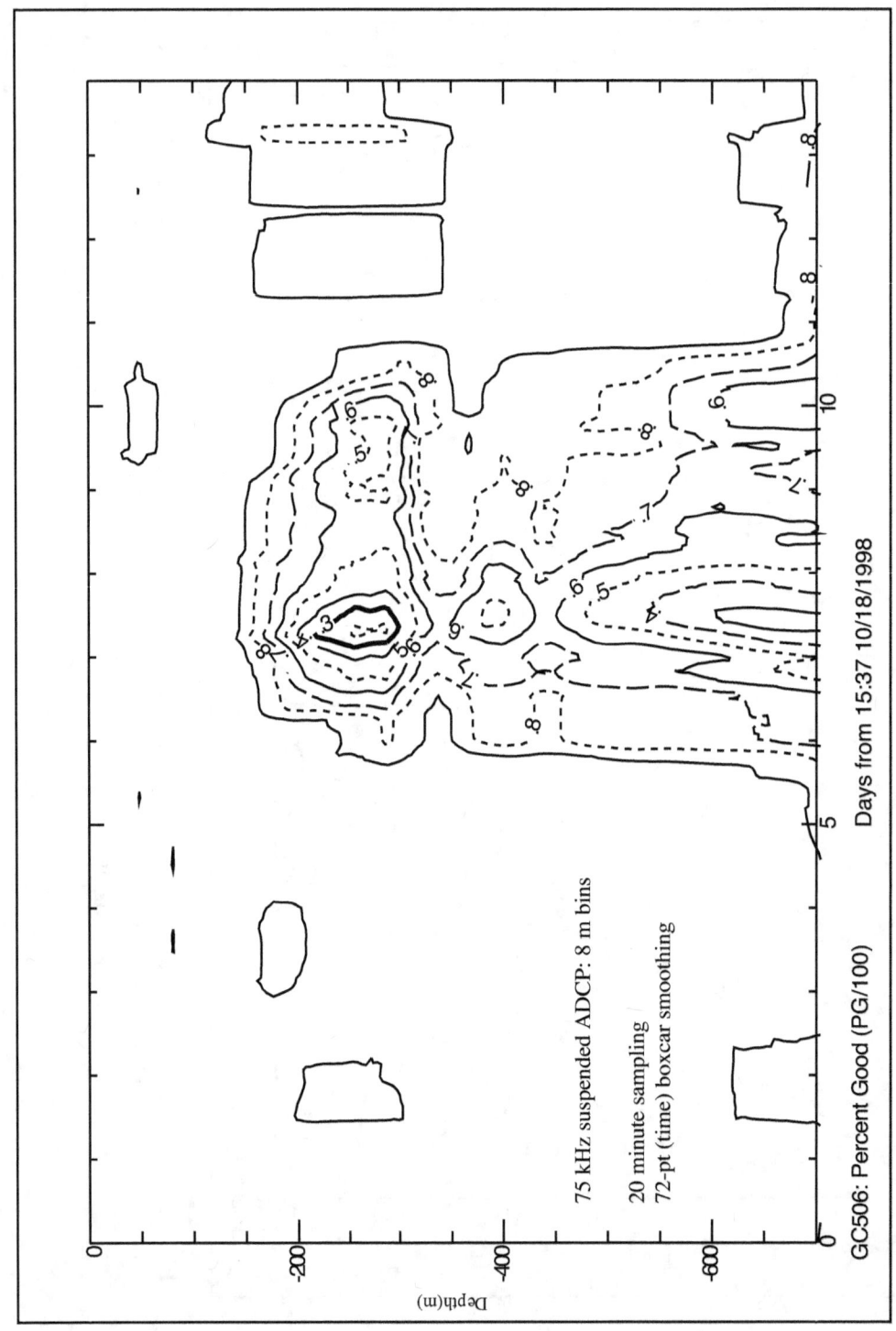

Figure 3.1.10-3. Contours of percentage of good pings per sampling interval versus depth and time at same location as Figure 3.1.10-2. Contour interval is 0.1. Data are courtesy of Texaco/Chevron.

208 cm·s^{-1} (6.4 feet·s^{-1}) at a depth of approximately 175 m (575 ft) (Figure 3.1.11-1). Note the English units of measure in this figure. The time between profiles is roughly one hour, but there is no available information on averaging interval or number and spacing of depth bins. Plots of vertical and error velocity show characteristic increases associated with inhomogeneous flow (Figure 3.1.11-2). Burlington no longer has the original data (it was erased from the hard drive after images were made).

The SSH field (Figure 3.1.11-3) during this jet showed a complicated pattern of highs and lows. The Loop Current was seen extending north, intruding into DeSoto and Mississippi Canyons, and even onto the eastern Texas-Louisiana shelf near the location of the measurements. This large northern extension of the Loop Current ultimately separated from the Loop Current in October 1999 and became a major Loop Current Eddy (Eddy Juggernaut). We note that the jet occurred at a bend in the SSH front and may indicate the possibility of a frontal instability (see Sections 4.4 and 5.1).

The AVHRR SST imagery (Figure 3.1.11-4) shows a nearly uniform surface temperature, typical of the summer months in the Gulf of Mexico. Cool filaments in the central Gulf are likely due to cloud cover.

Confidence in the ADCP data during this deployment is low. No digital version of these data is available for analysis and quality control, particularly lacking are beam correlations and echo intensities, as well as specifics about the deployment are unavailable.

3.2 ADCP Instrumentation Issues

3.2.1   Structural Interference

As can be surmised in the discussion of ADCP observations in section 3.1, the deployment design and placement of the instrument with respect to the platform structure are important. Improper deployment practices or instrument placement can seriously affect data quality. Acoustic Doppler profiling instruments are designed to measure currents by combining the return signals of multiple acoustic beams arranged in a fixed angle relative to the vertical axis. For 75 kHz instruments, this angle is typically 20°. The nominal range of a moored 75-kHz instrument is roughly 500 m. Therefore, when deployed in a downward-looking configuration; any object within a 182-m horizontal radius of the instrument has the potential to interfere with the emitted acoustic signal. Because many objects, e.g., risers, anchor cables, or drilling casings, are routinely hung from drill ships and production platforms, it is not unreasonable to believe that on occasion these structures pass into the acoustic beam's footprint.

If the specific location of structures hung off the platform are known prior to the instrument's deployment, a number of measures can be implemented to minimize the interference. From an observing point of view, placing the instrument as far from the platform as possible is the most desirable solution. This solution usually requires a completely separate mooring line for the instrumentation and is usually the most costly measure. In addition, platform operators do not particularly like the burden of worrying about an additional hazard (the mooring line) becoming

47

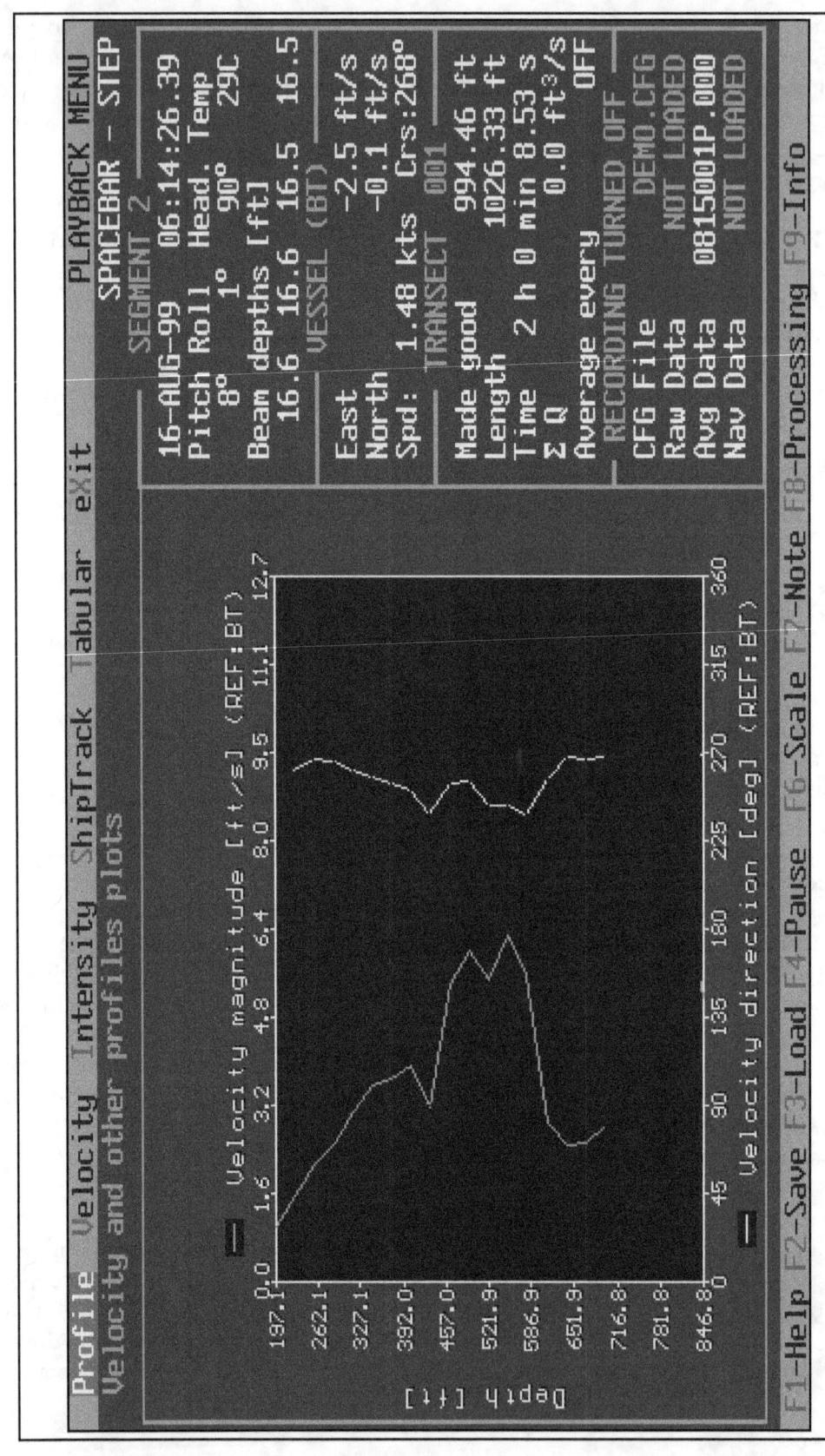

Figure 3.1.11-1. Screen image of ADCP control screen on 0614 UTC 16 Aug 1999 for EW913 case showing profile of speed and direction versus depth. Time is during maximum jet speed. Note English measurement units. Data courtesy Burlington.

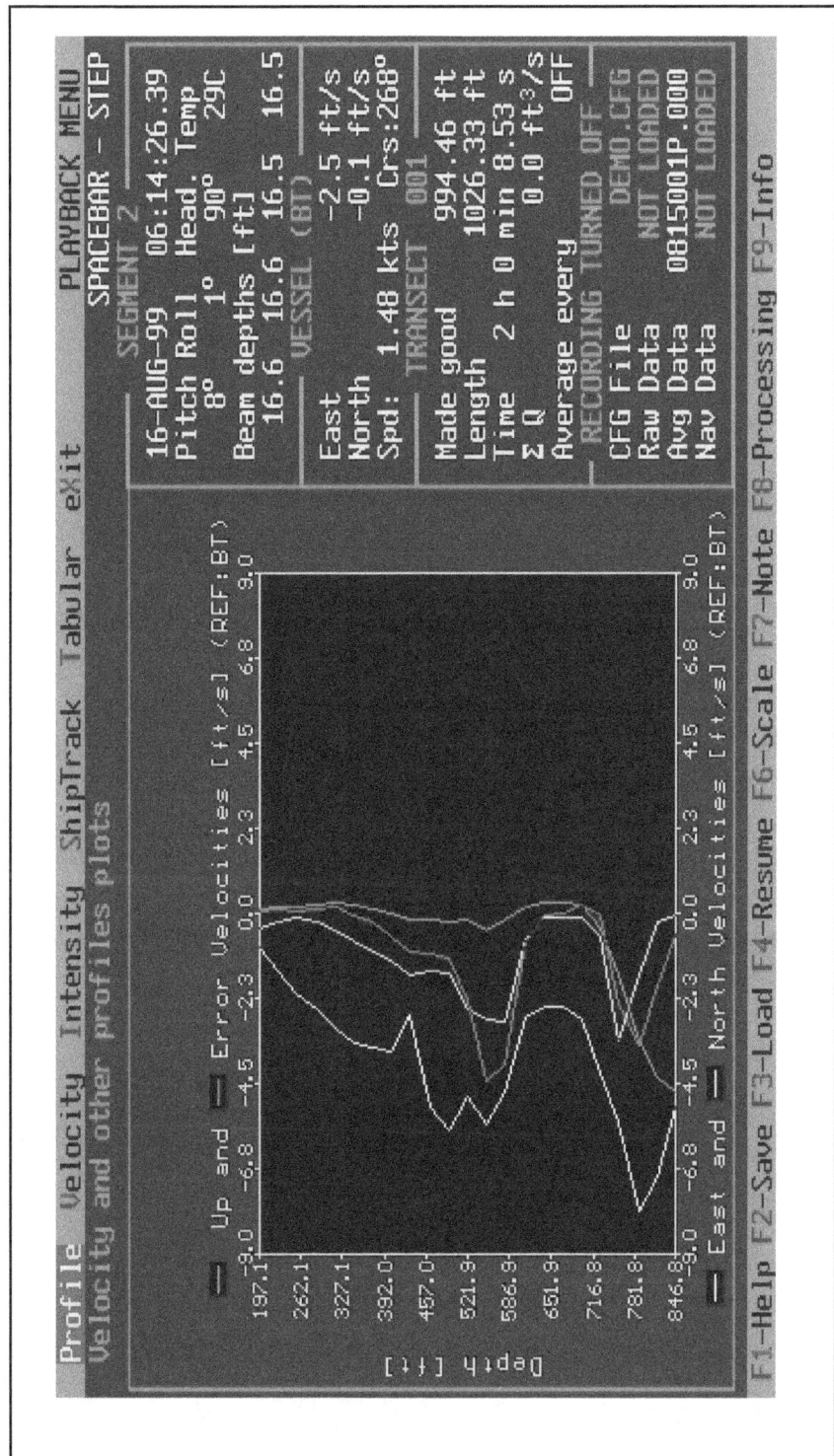

Figure 3.1.11-2. Screen image of ADCP control screen on 0614 UTC 16 Aug 1999 for EW913 case showing profiles of vertical (blue) and error (red) velocities (ft/s) versus depth. Time is during maximum jet speed. Note English measurement units. Data courtesy Burlington.

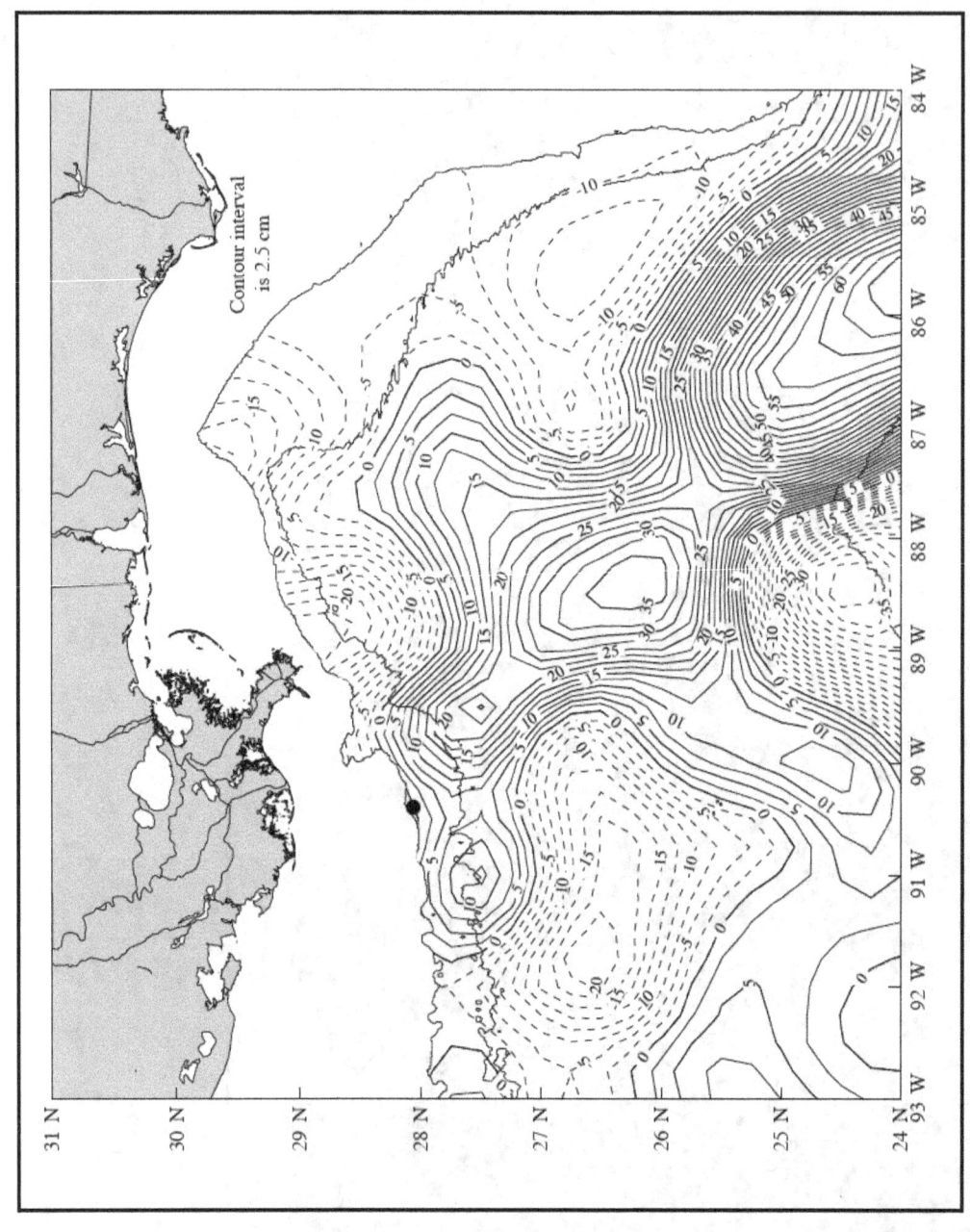

Figure 3.1.11-3. Sea-surface height field from satellite altimeter data for 16 Aug 1999 for EW913 case (dot). The 200 and 1000-m isobath contours are shown. [Data provided by Robert R. Leben, University of Colorado; plot provided courtesy of Ann Jochens, TAMU.]

50

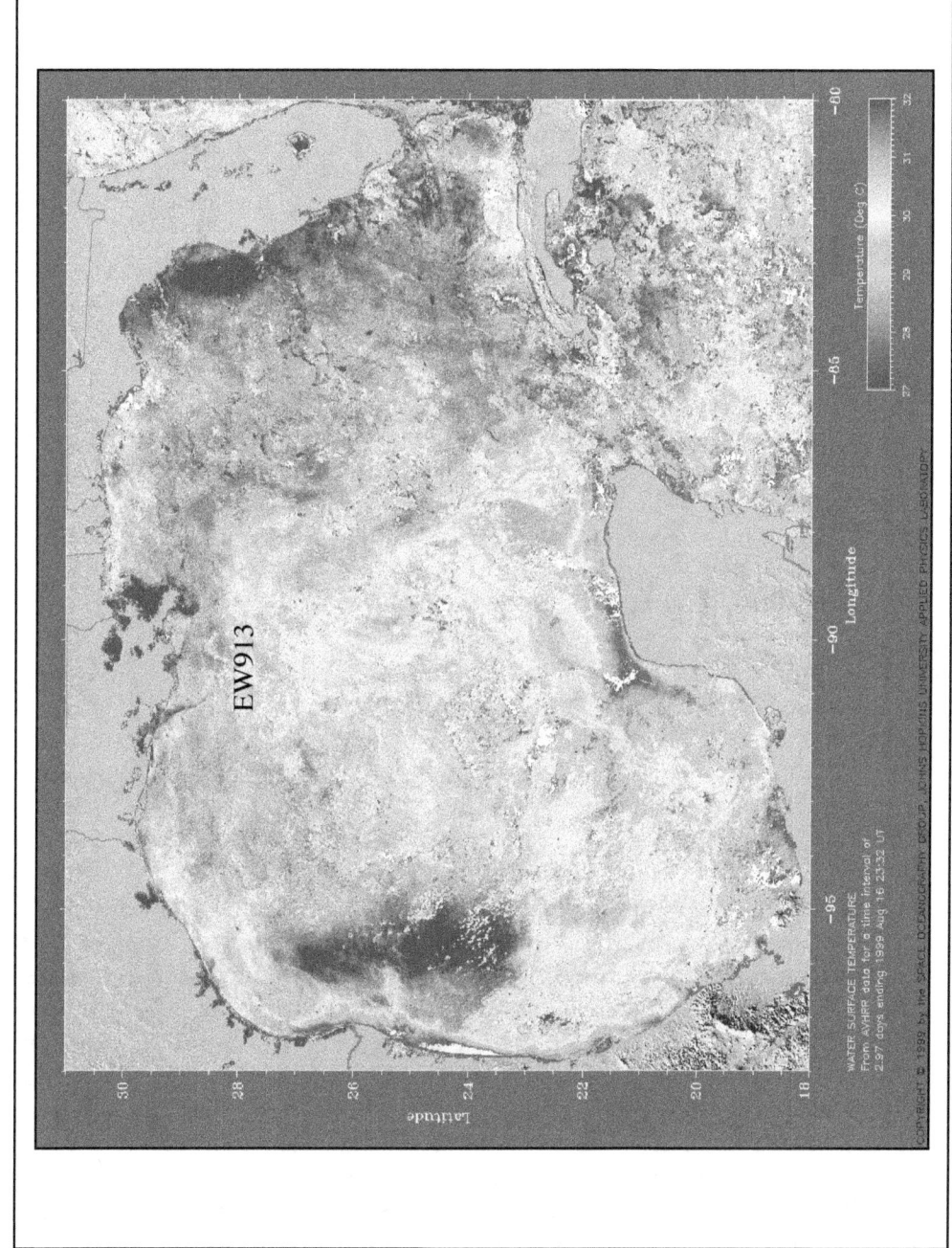

Figure 3.1.11-4. AVHRR image of sea-surface temperature of the Gulf of Mexico on 16 Aug 1999 (EW913 case). Image is an average of 7 images averaged over a 2-day period. Data courtesy of Johns Hopkins Applied Physics Laboratory.

51

entangled with platform risers, cables, or drill strings. Because the current observations are low priority compared to platform safety, the alternative is to place the instrumentation on the structure.

This however has additional drawbacks as well. Platform managers do not want instrumentation to interfere with platform operation. Therefore, locations where instrumentation is allowed are usually in inaccessible and undesirable places on the structure. Typically, this can be in a moon pool of the ship or on the outside jacket of a tension leg or spar. Because these structures influence the flow around the platform, the current measurements are usually contaminated to varying degrees. The radius of the instrumentation footprint usually assures that the platform structure or drilling operation will eventually interfere with the current measurements.

One solution commonly used it to intentionally configure the placement of the instrument so that one of the four acoustic beams is pointing directly at an existing drill string or riser. This acoustic beam is then turned off and not used when determining current speed and direction. This solution has the advantage of eliminating the potential interference of a known object. However, the instrument then has only three beams left to determine the horizontal and vertical components of velocity. A three-beam solution has reduced quality compared with a four-beam solution. Further, the four-beam solution includes a measure of the amount of inhomogeneity of the horizontal flow field in the form of the error velocity; something not available using a three-beam solution. The effects of inhomogeneity will be discussed more in Section 3.2.2.

3.2.2 Homogeneous Flow Assumption

The acoustic systems commonly used by scientists and industry to measure current velocity use a combination of the returned signals of four acoustic beams to estimate the flow field around the instrument. A fundamental assumption for the proper operation and accurate estimation of current magnitude is that the flow be homogeneous, i.e., uniform, in the path of all four acoustic beams (Gordon, 1996).

Figure 3.2.2-1 demonstrates how velocity is estimated using trigonometric relationships between the acoustic beam configuration and the flow field. For simplicity, we consider here only one component of horizontal velocity and vertical velocity at one fixed depth. The water velocity is estimated by emitting an acoustic pulse from the instrument. The acoustic pulse is then scattered by suspended particles in the water column. Some of the scattered acoustic pulse is reflected back in the direction of the instrument. The transducer then analyzes the returned acoustic signal. Because particles embedded in the water column are assumed to be traveling with the same speed as the water that carries them, they will have a velocity relative to the fixed instrument. This relative velocity will cause a shift in frequency of the returned signal that is proportional to the speed of the scatterer, i.e., a Doppler shift. By measuring the Doppler shift of the scattered acoustic signal at different times, a profile of the Doppler shift along a straight-line path from the instrument can be estimated. The Doppler shift is than translated into a velocity along the path. This velocity, termed the radial velocity, is the projection of the actual velocity along the radial path. By combining the radial components of two acoustic beams that are set at a fixed angle relative to each other, the horizontal and vertical velocity components can be estimated using the following transformation equations:

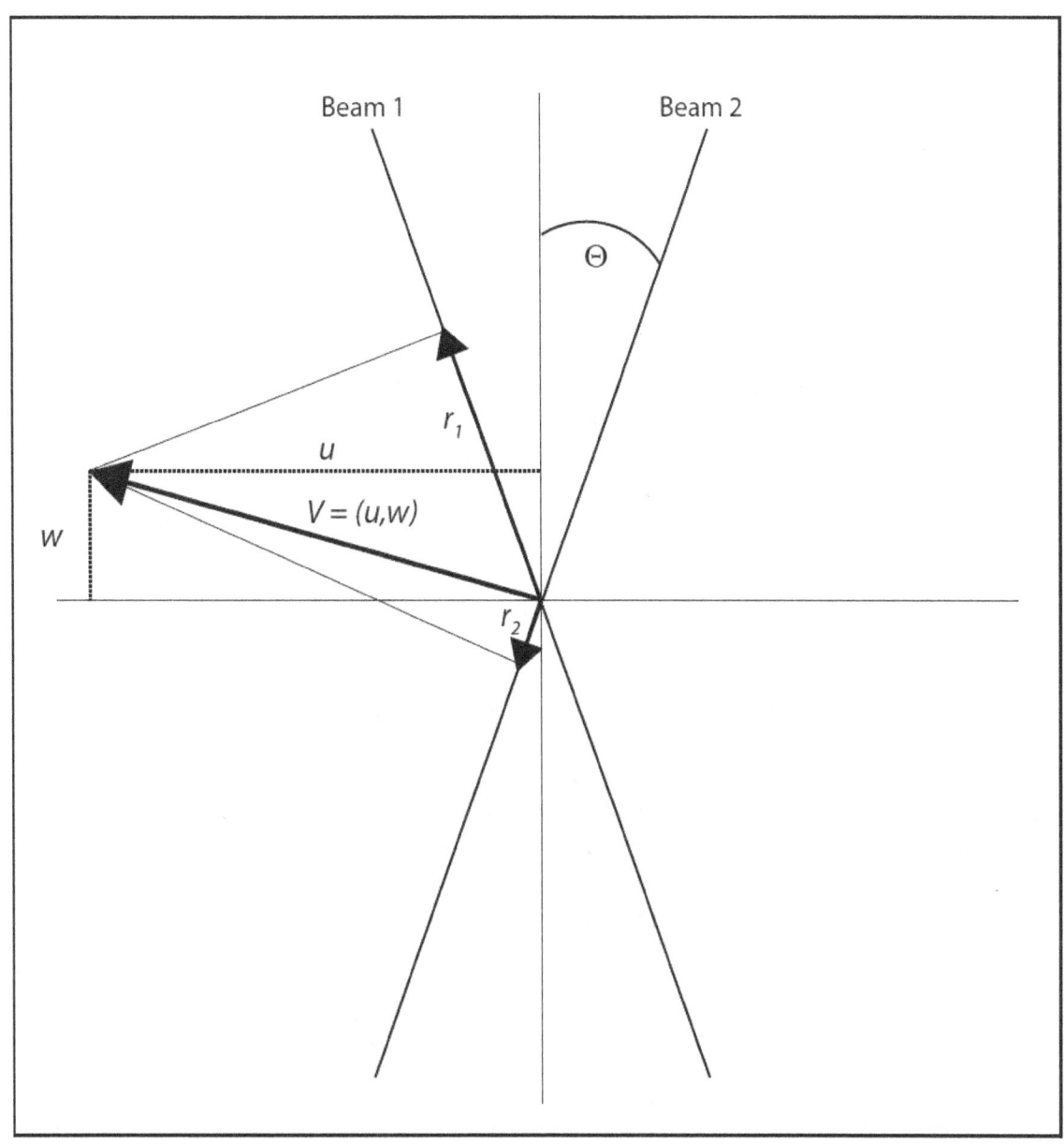

Figure 3.2.2-1. Schematic of projection of two-dimensional velocity (u, w) vector onto acoustic radial lines (beams 1 and 2). Equation 1 shows relationship between current velocity V and radial velocities (r_1 and r_2) for homogeneous case.

$$u = \left(\frac{r_2 - r_1}{2}\right)\csc(\Theta),$$

$$w = \left(\frac{r_2 + r_1}{2}\right)\sec(\Theta). \tag{1}$$

Here, r_1 and r_2 are the radial velocity along each beam (at a given depth), Θ is the angle of the beam relative to the vertical axis, and u and w are the horizontal and vertical velocities of the flow, respectively. The v component of horizontal velocity would be determined using two additional beams oriented perpendicular to the first pair of beams. This would result in a redundant measure of vertical velocity if the assumption of homogeneous flow is satisfied. The internal processing algorithms of the instrument are usually set to report the mean vertical velocity and the error velocity. The error velocity is defined as the difference in the two vertical velocity components. For homogeneous flow, the error velocity is necessarily zero. However, for inhomogeneous flow the error velocity is a useful built-in measure of the magnitude of the inhomogeneity.

If the flow is inhomogeneous, i.e., the flow is not the same in each beam, then Eqns. 1 are not valid. However, the internal processing algorithms of the instrument will nevertheless apply these equations to the measured radial velocities to produce a velocity estimate. If the inhomogeneity is extreme, the resulting velocity estimates can be especially peculiar.

We can demonstrate potential problems encountered with an inhomogeneous field by prescribing different velocities seen in two acoustics beams and transforming the velocities to radial velocities along the beam path. The transformation equations for this are:

$$r_1 = \left(-u_1 \sin(\Theta) + w_1 \cos(\Theta)\right),$$

$$r_2 = \left(u_2 \sin(\Theta) + w_2 \cos(\Theta)\right). \tag{2}$$

Where the subscripts 1 and 2 refer to the velocities seen in each of the two beams. This is represented schematically in Figure 3.2.2-2. The general form for the computed current velocity based on non-uniform flow in the two beams is given by:

$$u = \left(\frac{u_1 + u_2}{2}\right) + \left(\frac{w_1 - w_2}{2}\right)\cot(\Theta),$$

$$w = \left(\frac{w_1 + w_2}{2}\right) + \left(\frac{u_1 - u_2}{2}\right)\tan(\Theta). \tag{3}$$

The second terms are clearly the error in the estimated mean u and w produced by ignoring the inhomogeneity of u and w. We can test this by prescribing current velocities in the two beams and then use Eqns. 3 to simulate the instrument processing and determine the velocity components using the homogeneous assumption. It is readily seen that inhomogeneous flow in one component can produce spurious estimates in the other component. As an extreme example,

54

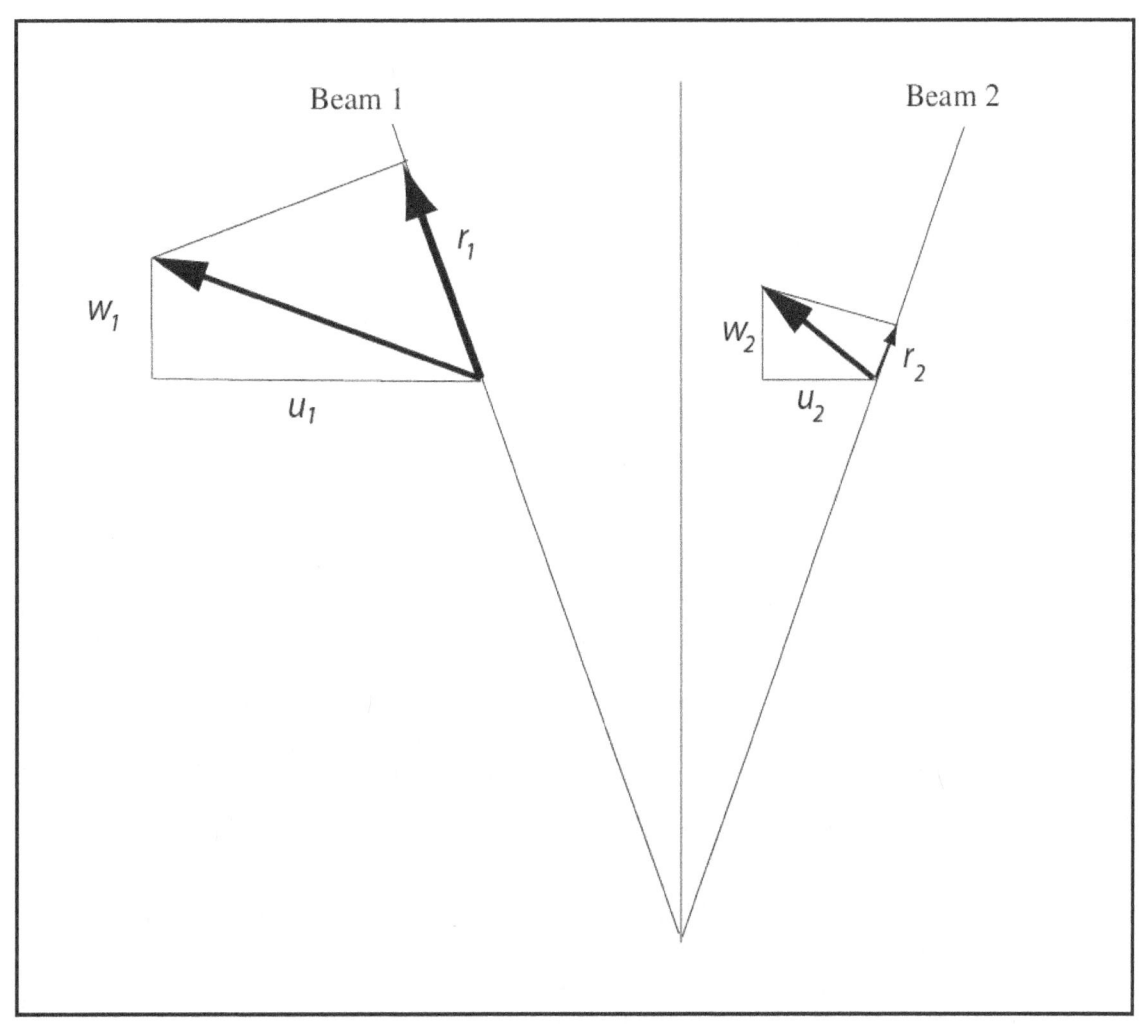

Figure 3.2.2-2. Schematic of projections of two-dimensional current velocity for nonhomogeneous case. Transformation equations are given in Eq. 2.

consider the initial velocity seen in beams one and two to be purely horizontal and of equal magnitude, but directed in opposite directions. Then after using the above transformation equations, the resulting vertical velocity will be estimated at 36% of the original horizontal speed magnitude. The computed horizontal speed will be zero, the mean of the two actual horizontal components.

The same type of result is found if the initial velocity is purely vertical and oppositely directed, i.e., upward in one beam and downward in the other. The computed horizontal speed will then be 2.75 times the vertical speed magnitude. The computed vertical component is zero.

It is not surprising then that inhomogeneous flow can have a profound effect on the measured current velocity. However, this result is not new. The instrument's operating manual clearly stresses the importance of homogeneous flow and how error velocity can be used to quantify the amount of inhomogeneity. Others have reported similar finding when using ADCPs to measure turbulent flow (Nystrom et al. 2002). We also point out that in the many tens of thousands of instrument hours of acoustic current profilers deployed in the deep ocean, we have found only 11 cases totaling several days where perhaps inhomogeneous flow substantially affected data quality. Therefore, the result is a testament of the instrument's utility in an oceanic environment.

The unusually large vertical and error velocities, some as high as 25 cm·s^{-1}, estimated in some of the current measurements taken during jet events confirms that the processes occurring at the time of the jet are associated with inhomogeneous flow. Further, the spatial scale of the inhomogeneity are at least on the order of 170 m, i.e., the distance between beams at roughly 250 m from the instrument where the jets are occurring. We stress that something is causing the inhomogeneity in that a significant event is occurring at these depths. However, because of the internal processing of the instrument, which assumes homogeneous flow, the resulting velocity estimates are not representative of the true flow field. The inhomogeneity can be caused by a number of mechanisms, which include: platform thrusters, naturally occurring turbulence in the water column, turbulence caused flow around the platform, or internal wave motions.

Instrument tilt can exacerbate the situation as the volume of water ensonified changes with the angle of inclination. The volume ensonified at a given depth increases with larger angles. The internal processing algorithms do account for tilt by applying different return acoustic travel times to each beam. However, if spatially small-scale processes are present, the ensonified volume may have an effect on the measurements.

Several measures can be implemented to minimize the effects that the inhomogeneous flow has upon the measurements. These include:

a. Collect single ping data. This would allow the analyst to identify the structure of the inhomogeneity rather than speculating from an averaged product.
b. Collect data in beam coordinates. This would allow for the analysis of radial velocities before they are transformed into earth coordinates.
c. Transform to earth coordinates during post-processing. Single ping radial velocities that are suspect can be eliminated and greatly improve overall data quality.

A more drastic, but more costly, remedy can be to equip the instrument with an additional fifth transducer that measures vertical velocity directly.

4. MODEL STUDIES

We now discuss the analyses of several general circulation numerical model outputs made available to the Study. The numerical models include the University of Colorado Princeton Ocean Model (CUPOM), the Princeton Regional Ocean Forecasting System (PROFS), the Navy Layered Ocean Model (NLOM), and idealized model output provided by Accurate Environmental Forecasting.

4.1 CUPOM Analysis

We first examined hourly CUPOM output with full vertical resolution at 134 locations in the northern Gulf of Mexico. We termed these "Probe" locations. Other sets of model output examined included full-resolution cross-shelf grids of locations (virtual arrays) similar to closely spaced arrays of moorings and full horizontal and vertical resolution grids at 6-hr time steps for selected regions. The latter were used: to prepare 3-D animations, to investigate horizontal scales, and to examine the relationship of jet events to topography and to the Loop Current and its eddies. A summary of CUPOM products is given in Table 4.1-1.

Table 4.1-1. CUPOM 1993-1999 Products.

Horizontal	Vertical	Temporal	Parameters
Whole Gulf	Sea Surface	3-hourly	SSH, Tx, Ty, U, V, T, S
Whole Gulf	Sea Surface, 50, 250, 500, 1000, 1500, 2000m, & Bottom	daily	SSH, Tx, Ty, U, V, T, S
Whole Gulf	Surface relative to 500, 1000, & 2000m	daily	Dynamic height
Deep Water Region	24 sigma levels	6-hourly	U,V,T,S
7 Cross-shelf sections (S of 26°N)	24 sigma levels	6-hourly	U,V,T,S
7 Cross-shelf Sections (N of 26°N)	24 sigma levels	hourly	U,V,T,S
5 Cross-shelf Sections (N of 26°N)	24 sigma levels	daily*	U,V,T,S
5 Along-isobath Sections (200, 500, 1000, 2000, 3000m isobaths)	24 sigma levels	hourly	U,V,T,S
134 Select Locations	24 sigma levels	hourly	U,V,T,S
57pt (3x19) grid	24 sigma levels	daily*	U,V,T,S

* Hourly output unavailable

59

We examined outputs of the CUPOM model at model probe locations (P13, P39, P71, and P108). Model output from probe locations are hourly at every vertical level. Speed contours plotted on depth versus time axes were examined for subsurface jet-like phenomena. The four probe locations were in the vicinity of the nine observational jet candidates and at comparable water depths and placement over the slope. Vertical current structure indicating subsurface currents was present throughout the record. However, the temporal duration of the subsurface features found in the model were typically much longer (2-6 days or longer) than those seen in observations (one-third to 2 days). Also, the high-speed current cores in the model were generally higher in the water column (150-250 m) than for the observations (200-400 m).

We have designed virtual current meter arrays using the Princeton Regional Ocean Forecasting System (PROFS) model output (data courtesy L. Oey, Princeton University) and the University of Colorado Princeton Ocean Model (CUPOM) to investigate the time and space scales and frequency of occurrence of subsurface jets from models.

Figure 4.1-1 shows the locations of the virtual moorings from each model. The outputs of the PROFS model were limited to probe locations extracted from the full model run. The model outputs are available at three-hour intervals during the period 1997 through 1999 with full vertical resolution and from both non-assimilated and assimilated runs. The PROFS virtual array locations were chosen to be in the vicinity of the jet candidates summarized in Table 3.1-1. Jets from observations are depicted as stars in Figure 4.1-1; CUPOM locations are depicted as triangles along 88°W and 90°W. PROFS array probes, depicted as filled circles, were in two general locations: one is centered at 88°W and the other just west of 90°W. The locations were chosen to investigate across-and along-slope variability during jet occurrences. The full three years of both assimilated and non-assimilated runs were investigated.

The CUPOM outputs are available in several forms and provide more analysis flexibility. Full vertical and hourly resolution are available at longitude lines near 90°W and 88°W. The positions of the CUPOM virtual array are depicted as filled triangles in Figure 4.1-1. The array contains every available model grid point between the 1000- and 2000-m isobaths.

Contours of speed versus time and depth were examined from CUPOM probe locations during the full seven-year run to identify the best occurrences for study of jets in the CUPOM model. Four jet candidates were identified. These are summarized in Table 4.1-2.

Table 4.1-2. Model Jet Candidate Summary

Name	Date	Location
M1	17 May 1993	88°W
M2	14 August 1993	90°W
M3	20 March 1998	88°W and 90°W
M4	10 April 1998	90°W

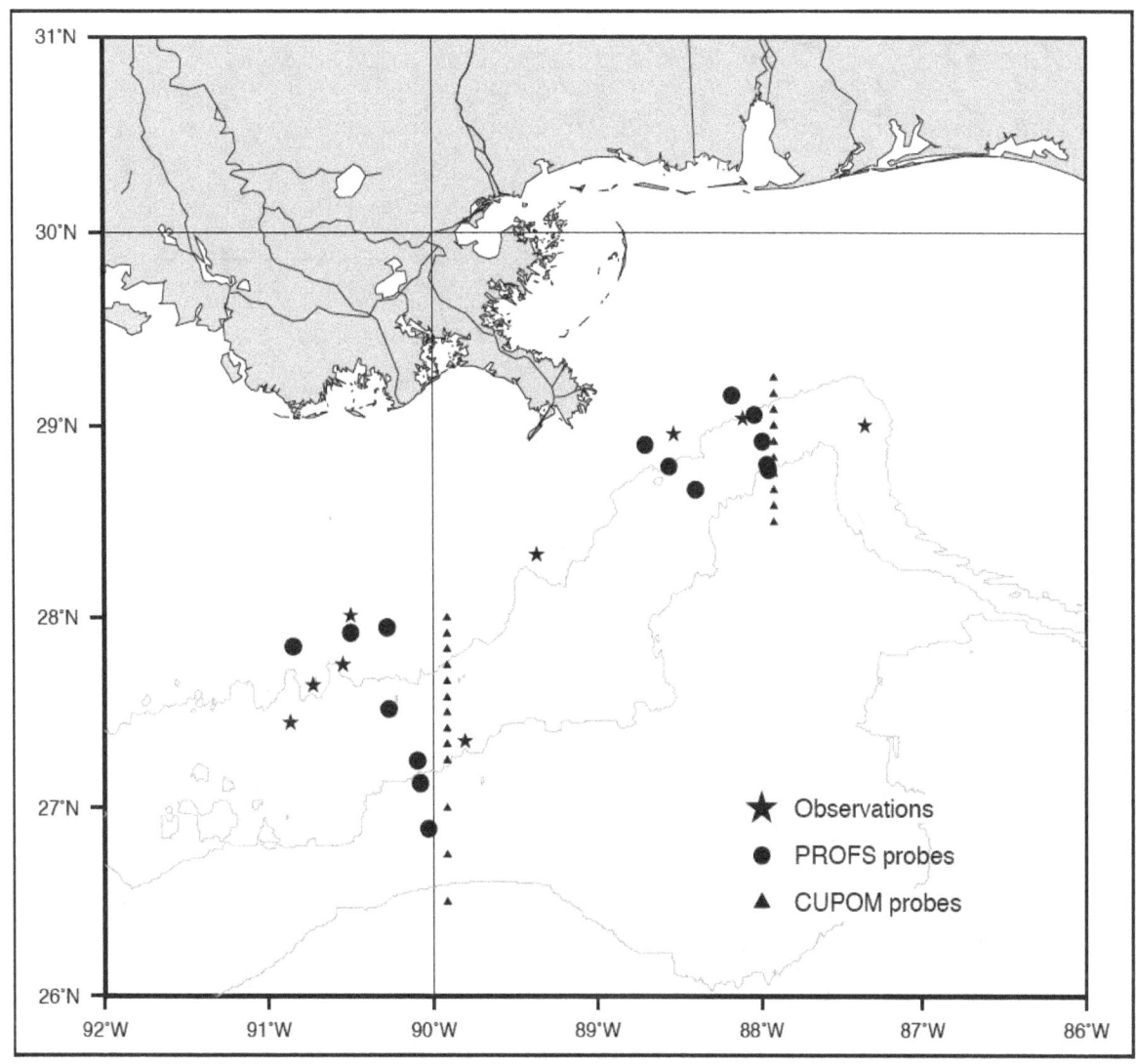

Figure 4.1-1. Map of north-central Gulf of Mexico south of Mississippi River delta showing locations of observed high-speed subsurface jets (stars) and virtual current meter arrays based on model outputs of PROFS model (circles) and CUPOM (triangles). The 1000, 2000, and 3000 m isobaths are shown.

The locations given in Table 4.1-2 represent the longitude line where the subsurface jets appear on the given date.

An example of the cross-slope variability of the M2 jet is shown in the sequence of plots in Figure 4.1-2. The panels of Figure 4.1-2 are arranged with north at the top of the page and south at the bottom. The center panel of Figure 4.1-2 shows speed contours versus depth and time (hours from 0000 1 January 1993) at 90°W, 27.5°N; the jet core is centered at 150 m at hour

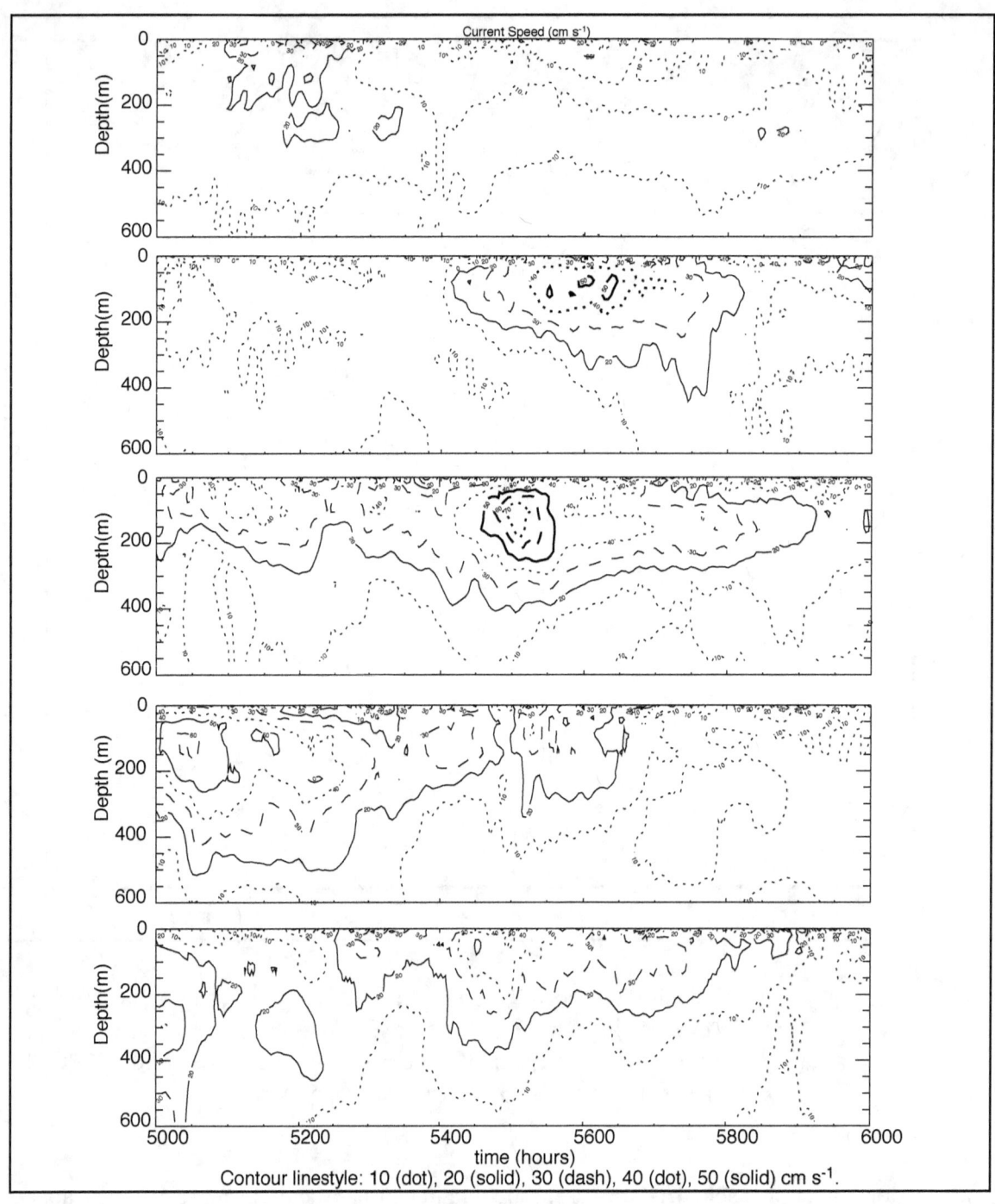

Figure 4.1-2. Contours of speed versus depth and time during subsurface event M2 seen in the CUPOM output at five locations along 90°W. Panels are arranged with northernmost location at top of page, southernmost at bottom. See Figure 4.1-1 for geographical locations of CUPOM output. Latitudes of panels are: 28°N (top), 27.75°N, 27.5°N (middle), 27.25°N, and 27°N (bottom).

5500. We can see in the top panel that there is no indication of the jet at 28°N. The jet peaks in speed at 27.5°N and then decreases in strength to the south and is gone by 27°N. Figures of current stick vectors at the same time and location as the contour plots shown in Figure 4.1-2 also were constructed and examined (not shown).

Another CUPOM model product is available with 6-hour temporal resolution and full horizontal and vertical resolution in the deepwater region of the north Gulf. This model product was analyzed to supplement the virtual current array shown in Figure 4.1-1. Specifically, computer animations of vector velocity were developed to depict flow in a volume of ocean during the time of the jets identified in Table 4.1-2. The three-dimensional computer animations of vector velocity along with sea surface height (to track eddy movement) allowed a more refined analysis of the spatial development of the jet and estimates of horizontal scales.

Examination of 3-D velocity animations described above and SSH (Figure 4.1-3) during jet M2 indicates that a Loop Current Eddy had broken off from the Loop Current several weeks prior to this jet and moved westward to the central Gulf of Mexico. As the Loop Current extended northward, a cyclonic feature developed over the northern slope at about 89°W, 28°N. A filament from the Loop Current then appeared to break free and form a small anti-cyclone at about 91°W, 26°N. This feature began to move north toward the cyclone on the slope. As the two features approached each other, a jet of high current speed was created between them. The jet appeared at approximately 250 m and seemed to propagate upward in the water column. Once near 150 m, this jet remained rather stationary between the two features with velocity oriented eastward along the slope. The lifetime of this jet was approximately 4 days and it was about 50 km in width, 75 km in length, and 150 m in vertical thickness. This jet may have resulted from the combined effects of the interaction of the Loop Current with bottom topography and eddy-eddy interaction.

Figure 4.1-4 shows the M2 jet from two different views. The upper panel is a plan view from above showing sea surface height (yellow) at 0.5 cm intervals, the 50 cm·s^{-1} isosurface (orange) and the horizontal velocity (blue). The view includes the topography of the shelf and slope. The lower panel is the mid-water view from the north looking south without topography. White squares in each panel mark the same location for reference. The white squares are located at the tail of a filament that grew from east to west in the region between the loop current and the region of cyclonic flow to the north and east of the filament.

Figure 4.1-5 shows contours of speed versus depth and time of CUPOM output during the M1 jet event. Speed contours in the upper three panels show subsurface current maxima between 100 and 200 m that exceed 50 cm·s^{-1}. Animations of the three-dimensional velocity field show that these maxima were associated with a large cyclonic circulation over the northeastern Gulf of Mexico. The jet is revealed as a filament, originating at the Loop Current, which impacted the West Florida Slope, turned cyclonically and flowed along the boundary of the DeSoto Canyon. The flow then turned southward and completed the circulation by joining with the eastward-flowing northern limb of the Loop Current.

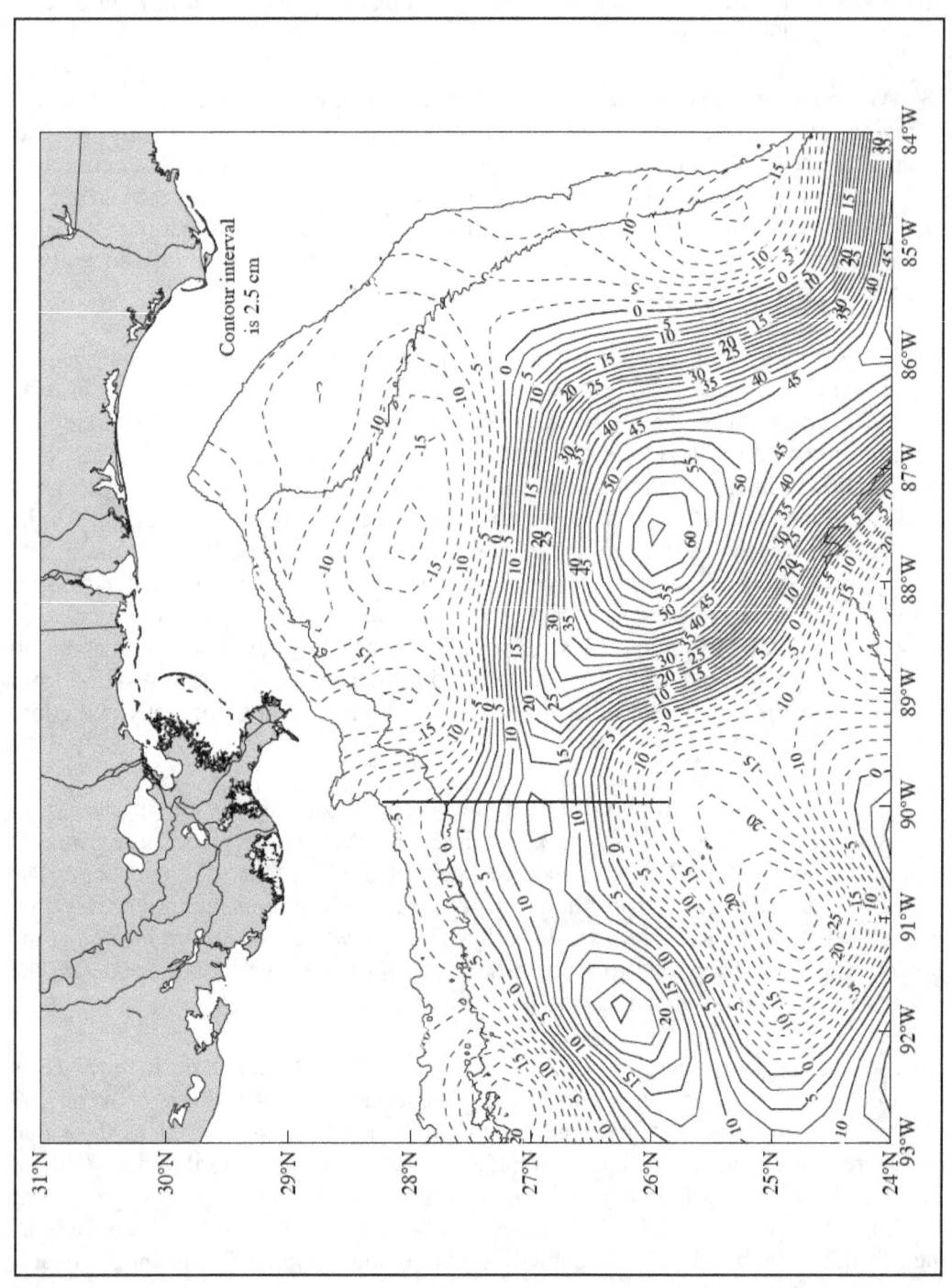

Figure 4.1-3. Sea-surface height field from satellite altimeter data for 17 May 1993 for M2 case. The 200- and 1000-m isobath contours are shown. Meridional line near 90°W indicates location of model output shown in Figure 4.1-2. [Data provided by Robert R. Leben, University of Colorado; plot provided courtesy Ann Jochens, TAMU.]

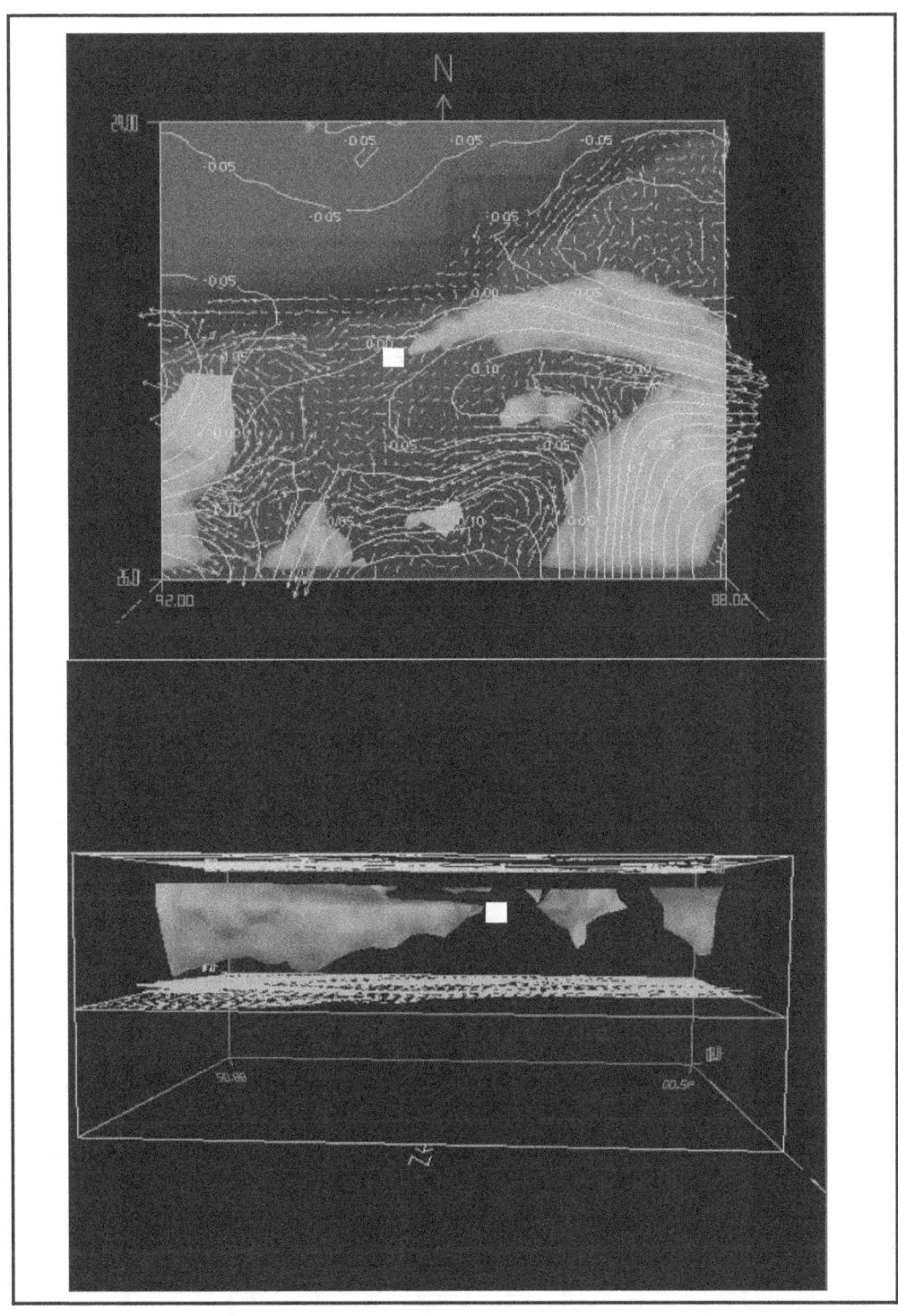

Figure 4.1-4. Three-dimensional view of M2 jet showing sea-surface height (yellow), the 50 cm·s⁻¹ isosurface (orange), and horizontal velocity (blue). Upper panel is plan view. Lower panel is view from the north looking south with the topography removed. The white squares mark the same location at the tail of the jet.

65

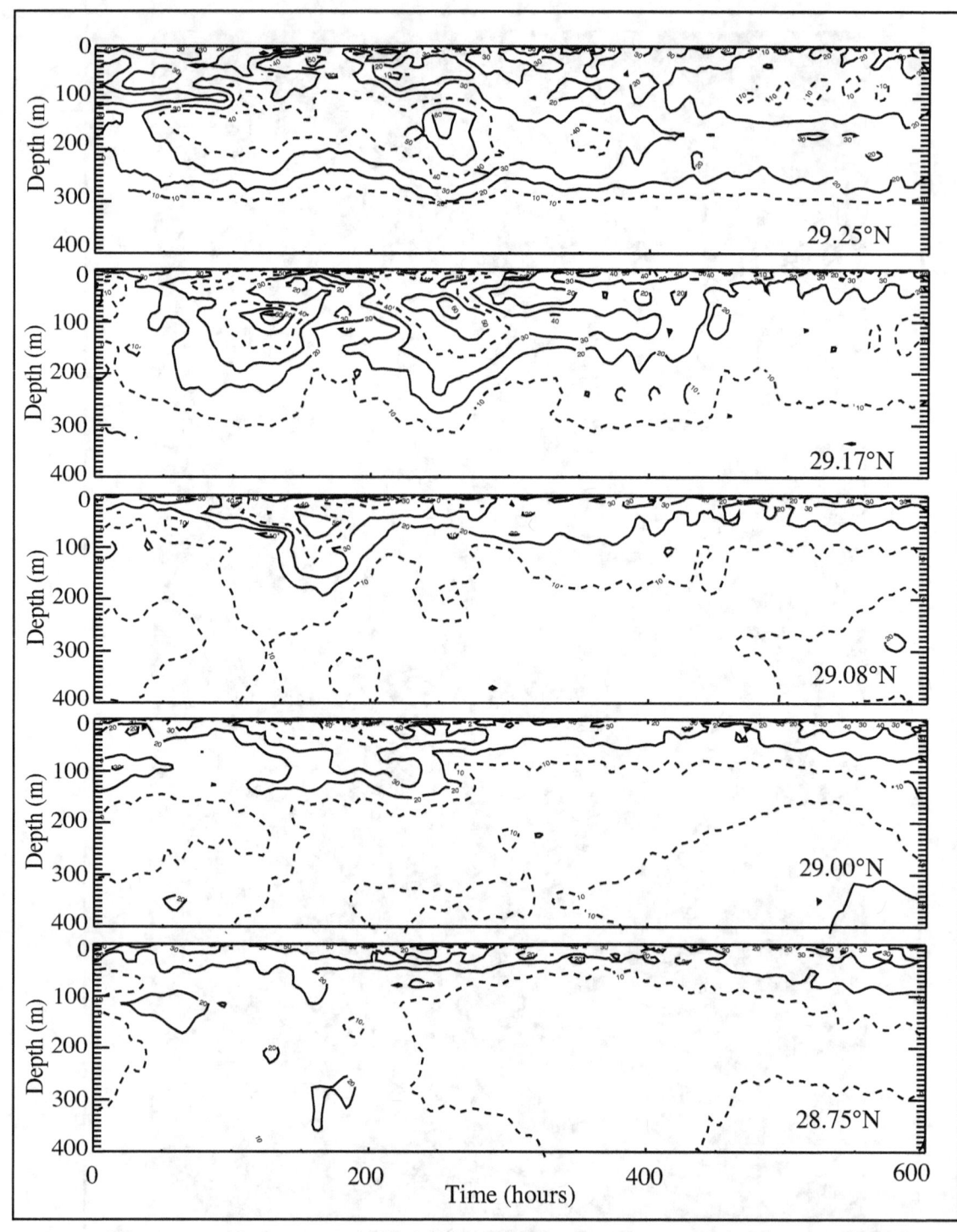

Figure 4.1-5. Contours of speed versus depth and time during subsurface event M1 seen in the CUPOM output at five locations along 88°W. Panels are arranged with northernmost location at top of page. Latitudes of panels are: 29.25°N, 29.17°N, 29.08°N, 29.00°N, 28.75°N. Contour interval is 10 cm·s^{-1}.

Figure 4.1-6 shows contours of speed versus depth and time for the M3 jet event. Speed contours in the upper four panels show subsurface maxima between 100 and 400 m exceeding 60 cm·s^{-1}. Animations of this event reveal circulation features similar to events M1 and M2. A large cyclonic circulation pattern is established in the northern Gulf as the Loop Current impacted the West Florida slope and turned cyclonically around the DeSoto Canyon region. The currents were intensified near topography and regions of convergence of multiple filaments.

CUPOM output well suited for examination of mid-water jets are hourly values at many levels through the water column. Before model runs were made, petroleum company representatives of the Eddy Joint Industry project and project personnel identified 134 locations as being of special interest or locations where current meter records were known (or believed) to exist. Model outputs consisting of hourly values of horizontal velocity components, temperature and salinity were saved at 24 levels in the vertical at each of those locations. Computer programs were written that compared the instantaneous values of speed averaged over levels between 50 and 100 m with instantaneous speed values at each level in the depth range 200 to 500 m at the same location and time. Only stations with water depths greater than 500 m were considered.

At each probe location current throughout the 7-year CUPOM output were examined for jets. The criteria used were that model speeds anywhere in the depth range 200-500 m exceeded 45 cm·s^{-1} and exceeded the vertically-averaged speed for levels in the depth range 50-100 m. The 73 station locations where these test criteria were met are shown in Figure 4.1-7. The criteria were met for some locations in each of the seven years. In 1998, the criterion were met on a spatially widespread basis. The plot shows that the criteria were met at locations in the north-central Gulf of Mexico between 87W and 92W in water depths between 500 and 2000 m, however, some instances did occur in the north-western Gulf and on the West Florida Slope. It should be emphasized that of the 134 stations tested, most were in the north-central Gulf.

4.2 PROFS CGS and FGS Analysis

Figures 4.2-1a and 4.2-1b show contour plots of current speed versus time and depth at a site near lease block AT575 from the CGS version of the PROFS model. This probe was selected because a subsurface jet was observed at this site during June 1995. Following the passage of a Loop Current Eddy, the jet reached a peak speed of 55 cm·s^{-1} (approximately 1 knot). The model output have not been filtered other than decimation to three-hourly intervals prior to contouring.

Figure 4.2-1a shows speed contour from the run without data assimilation. The plot begins at day 250 (7 September 1997) and continues to day 450 (16 March 1998). Early in this period (days 250-300), the Loop Current Eddy El Dorado passed by the probe location. The LCE is evident as a surface-intensified feature penetrating to 200-m depth with maximum speeds exceeding 80 cm·s^{-1}. By day 350, the 20 cm·s^{-1} contours are above 100-m depth and signal the end of the eddy event. There is considerable diurnal variability of the speed contours throughout the records. Vertical oscillations of the 20 cm·s^{-1} speed contour span more than 200 m beginning around day 300. There were no instances of intense sub-surface jets at this station during this period; however, there were several occurrences of isolated internal wave trains of inertial period. For example, such a wave train is seen in Figure 4.2-1a at approximately 400-m depth and beginning

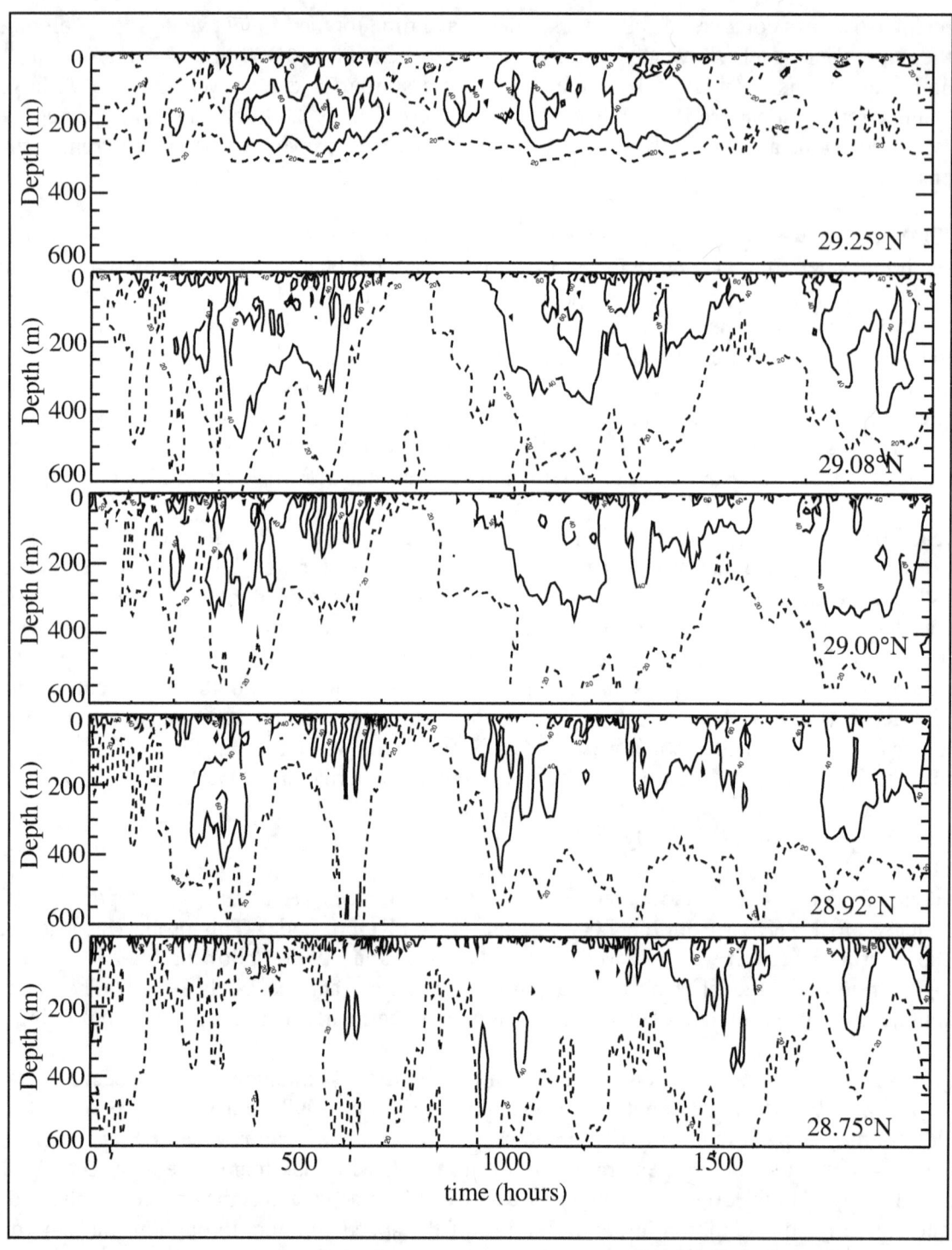

Figure 4.1-6. Contours of speed versus depth and time during subsurface event M3 seen in the CUPOM output at five locations along 88°W. Panels are arranged with northernmost location at top of page. Latitudes of panels are: 29.25°N, 29.17°N, 29.08°N, 29.00°N, 28.75°N. Contour interval is 20 cm·s [1].

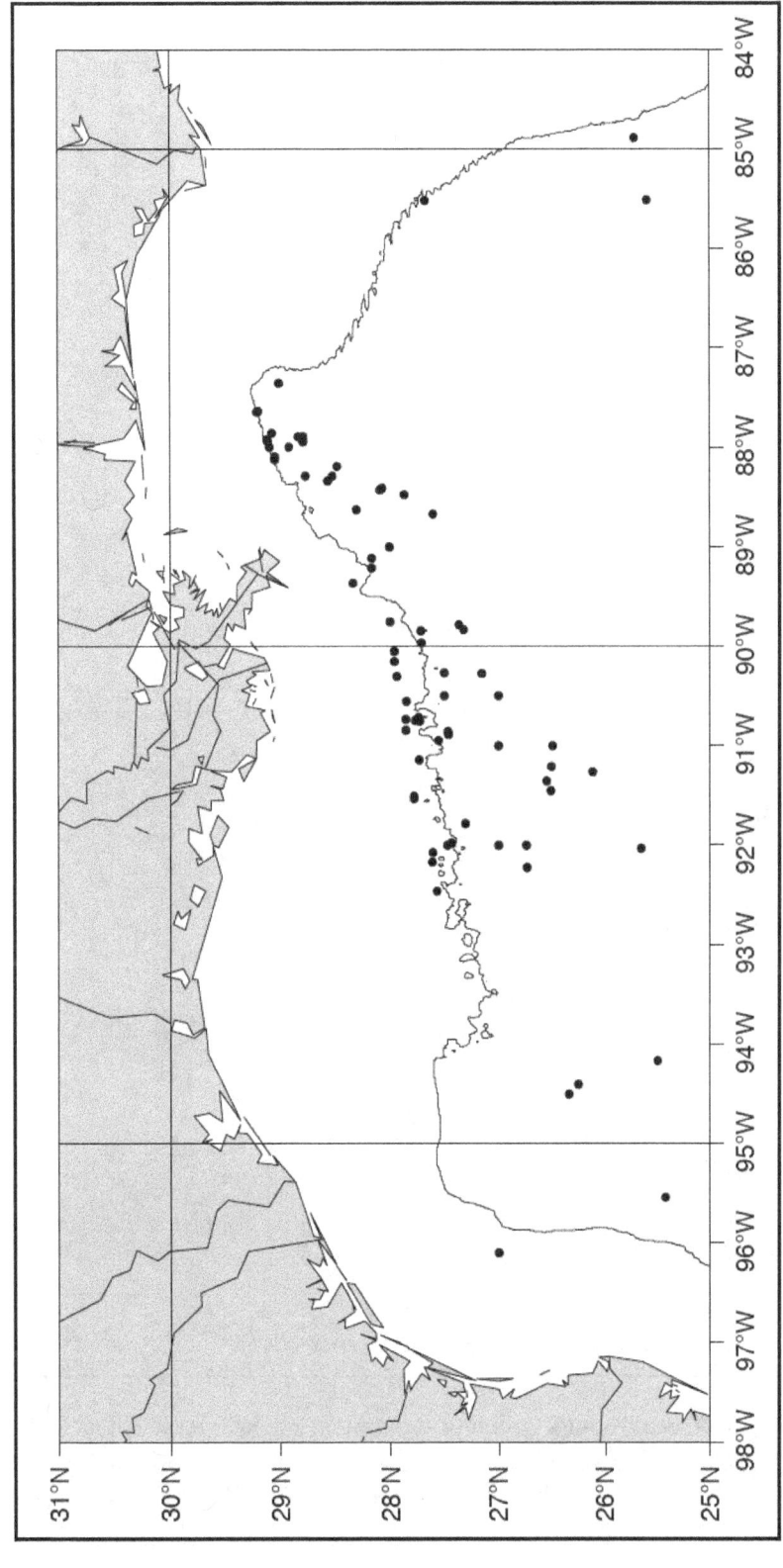

Figure 4.1-7. Locations of model stations where model speeds anywhere between 200 and 500 m exceeded both 45 cm·s⁻¹ and the vertically-averaged speed for levels in the depth range 50-100 m.

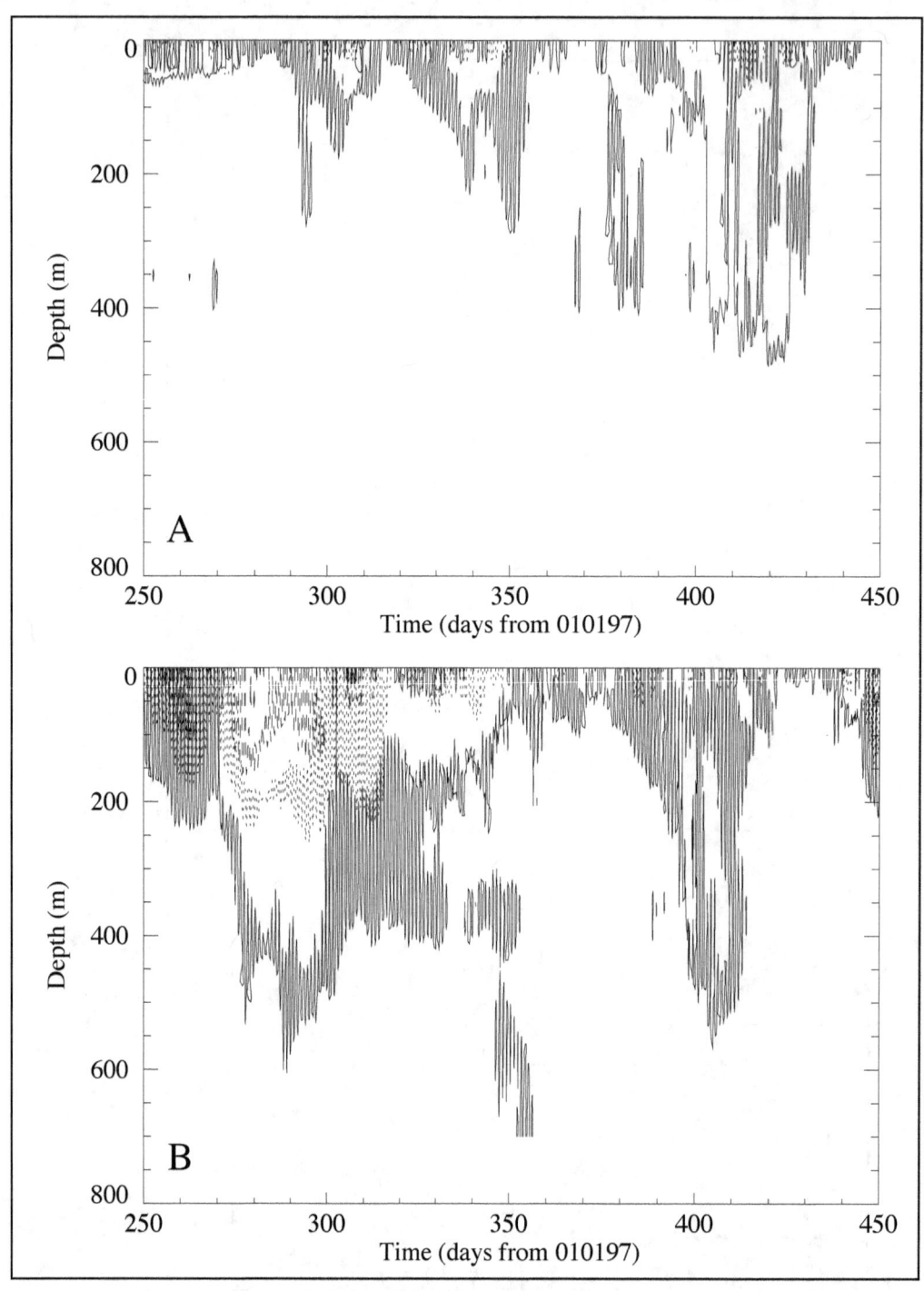

Figure 4.2-1. Current speed from PROFS model output at site near lease block AT575: a) no data assimilaiton, b) with data assimilation. PROFS model has 26 sigma levels. Contour interval is 20 cm·s^{-1} (solid=20 cm·s^{-1}; dotted=40 cm·s^{-1}; dash=60 cm·s^{-1}).

around day 335- and 550-m depth beginning around day 345. This wave train, with peak speeds of over 20 cm·s⁻¹, is likely related to the downward propagation of inertial energy associated with the passage of the Loop Current Eddy.

Figure 4.2-1b shows contours of current speed at the same dates and location as that of Figure 4.2-1a, however, this run was made with data assimilation. Evident in this figure are energetic currents that are confined mainly to the upper 50 m with little downward penetration of energy. Diurnal oscillation again dominate the contours, however, the 20 cm·s⁻¹ contour rarely dips below 300 m during days 1-900. The most pronounced period of energetic currents below 200 m is during days 400-420. However, there was no near-surface event during that time to link as a causal mechanism for the subsurface energetics.

The PROFS FGS output we received overlapped with the passage of Hurricane Georges in September 1998. This strong and intense storm passed through the eastern Gulf of Mexico and DeSoto Slope around 28 September. Current observations taken during the MMS-funded DeSoto Canyon Eddy Intrusion Study indicate the presence of a downward propagating inertial oscillation packet to at least depths of 500 m (Section 3.1.9). The packet reaches 500 m almost 14 days after the initial impact of the Hurricane in the region. We compared PROFS model output at similar depths to determine if the downward propagation of inertial energy is sufficiently accounted for in the model. Figure 4.2-2 shows time series of component velocity for observations (left) and model output (right). Raw near-surface currents speeds exceeded 200 cm·s⁻¹ while band-passed 72-m currents speeds exceed 35 cm·s⁻¹ based on observations; model near-surface currents are considerably weaker and peak at 10-15 cm·s⁻¹ at 70 m. At 500 m, model current amplitudes are about 5 cm·s⁻¹. Inertial energy in the model seems to be contained above the thermocline. The weak currents and lack of downward penetration of inertial energy may result because gridded winds fields were used to represent the hurricane, which tend to smooth the fields spatially and temporally. Also, damping between vertical layers can affect the downward propagation of inertial energy in the model.

A cluster of observed jet candidates is located near the 1000-m isobath near 91°W (Figure 3.1-1). Analysis of the assimilative version of the FGS PROFS output from January to June 1998 at lease block GC236 shows considerable kinetic energy in the midwater depths. The total water depth at the model station analyzed is 553 m. The time period overlaps with the jet described in Section 3.1.8.

Figure 4.2-3 (provided by Leo Oey) shows a time series of isotherm depth at this location and time. The upper 150 m is characterized by the annual cycle of heating and cooling. Below 150 m, shorter time scales characterize the variability. A signal with distinct 24-hour period is seen at all depths and levels. The 15°C isotherm has frequent vertical excursions of 100 m; the 5°C isotherm ranges from about 400 m to the bottom. Speed contours (Figure 4.2-3; middle) show midwater currents centered at 150 m that frequently exceed 55 cm·s⁻¹. These currents tend to persist for days and even weeks at a time. Strong inertial currents are also present throughout the record at all depths. The bottom panel of Figure 4.2-3 shows contours of the difference of speed between the subsurface and surface currents. Color contours represent the difference when it is

71

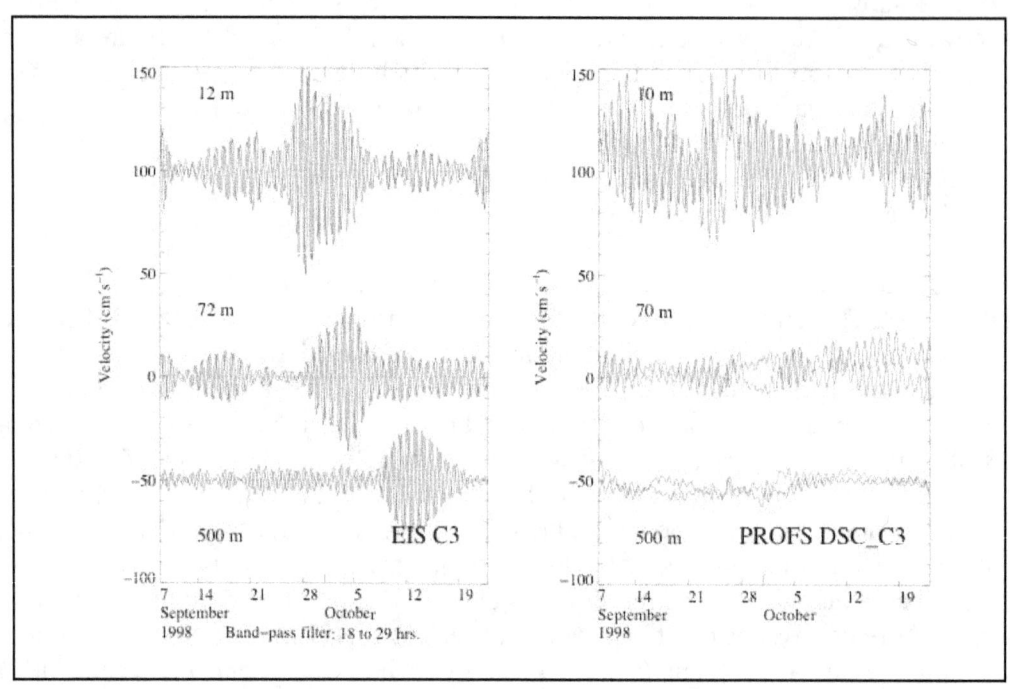

Figure 4.2-2. (Left) 18-29 hr band-pass filtered current velocity at 12, 72, and 500 m depths at the MMS Eddy Intrusion Study mooring C3 during Hurricane Georges. East-west component is black; north-south component is blue. (Right) Raw current component velocities taken from PROFS FGS model run at depths 10, 70, and 500 m. PROFS output courtesy of Dr. Leo Oey, Princeton University.

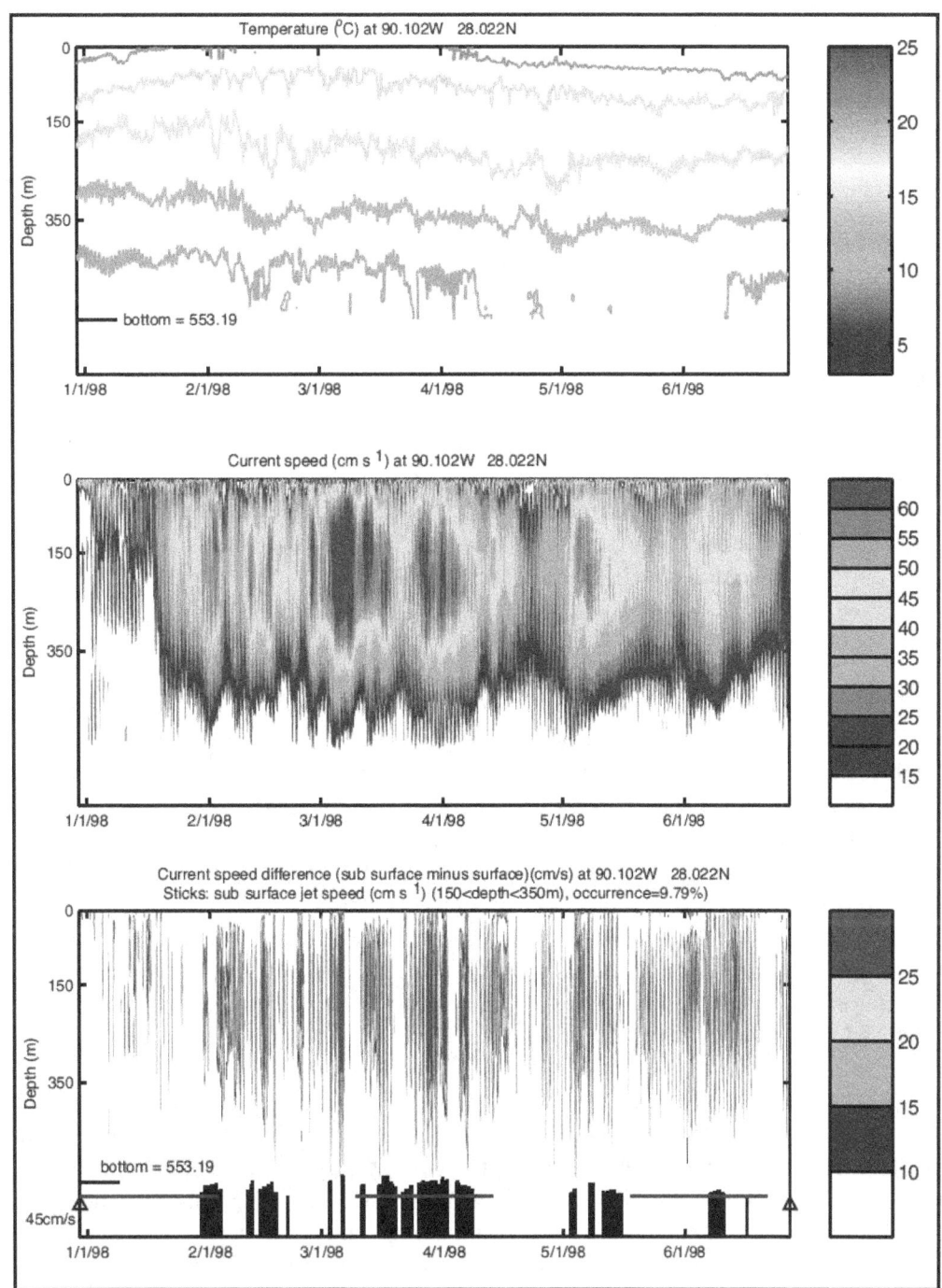

Figure 4.2-3. (Top) Depth of isotherm versus time from FGS version of PROFS model from model year 1 Jan 1998 through 30 Jun 1998. Bottom depth is 553.19 (Middle) Contours of speed versus depth and time. (Bottom) Difference of speed maximum between 150 and 300 m and surface speed versus depth and time. Output is taken at 90.10°W and 28.022°N and is near jet observed in lease block GC236 on 11 Apr 1998. Figure is provided by Leo Oey (Princeton University).

73

positive (subsurface greater than surface) and greater than 10 cm·s^{-1}. The vertical lines at the bottom of this panel indicate when currents between 150 and 350 m are greater than 45 cm·s^{-1}. The line length indicates the maximum velocity in this depth range.

A plan view of current at different depths on model date 11 April 1998 shows the regional circulation patterns at the time of the observed jet at GC236 (Figure 4.2-4). The northern limb of the Loop Current is in the southern part of the figure between 85°W and 86°W; a Loop Current Eddy is centered at 88°W, 25.5°N. A filament extending north from the Loop Current can be seen running north along the West Florida Shelf break (~200 m), turning west and crossing the DeSoto Canyon, and continuing west and unbroken to the Texas-Louisiana Shelf edge. The water depth under this filament is between 200 and 500 m. The subsurface intensification at 200 m (middle panel) is clearly associated with current features seen at 20 m. The features are not present at 800 m (bottom panel). This type of feature was also seen in the CUPOM outputs shown in Section 4.1. Because of the long temporal and spatial scales of these features we do not believe this to be the mechanism responsible for producing the jet events seen in the observations. However, we do not rule this out as a possible mechanism for producing subsurface intensified currents. A closely spaced (5 km) cross shelf-edge line of current moorings along 91°W would provide the necessary measurements to verify this numerical result.

4.3 NLOM Analysis

We received numerical output of the Navy Ocean Layered Model (NLOM) during August 1999. Outputs are courtesy of Tamara Townsend and William Jobst of the Naval Research Laboratory. The period was chosen because of the presence of an unusually large Loop Current Eddy (Eddy Juggernaut) impinging on the northern slopes of the Gulf of Mexico. This was also the time period in which observations indicated a sub-surface jet in lease block EW913 (Section 3.1.11). The outputs consisted of approximately 500 MB of animations and graphics. This version of NLOM is a 1/16° global operation product run daily by the Naval Oceanographic Office. The model incorporates the following forcing: atmospheric forcing from the Navy Operation Global Atmospheric Prediction System (NOGAPS) and the assimilation of sea surface temperature and altimeter data obtained via the NAVOCEANO Altimeter Data Fusion Center. More information concerning NLOM can be found at (http://www7320.nrlssc.navy.mil/global_nlom/index.html).

Figure 4.3-1 shows the NLOM sea surface height field on 1 August 1999. A Loop Current Eddy is seen centered at 90°W and 26.5°N. Figure 4.3-2 shows current vectors plotted over color contours of speed on 16 August 1999 at three model depth layers roughly centered at 80 (top), 400 (middle), and 600 (bottom) m. The middle panel showing layer 2 pictures some subsurface intensification of currents along the northern boundary of the eddy where it was interacting with the bathymetry. Currents are intensified in regions of convergence. There is also some indication of subsurface intensification southwest of the eddy. In general, however, the subsurface and near-surface currents seem linked. Note the change of contour interval and speed range in the bottom panel of Figure 4.3-2.

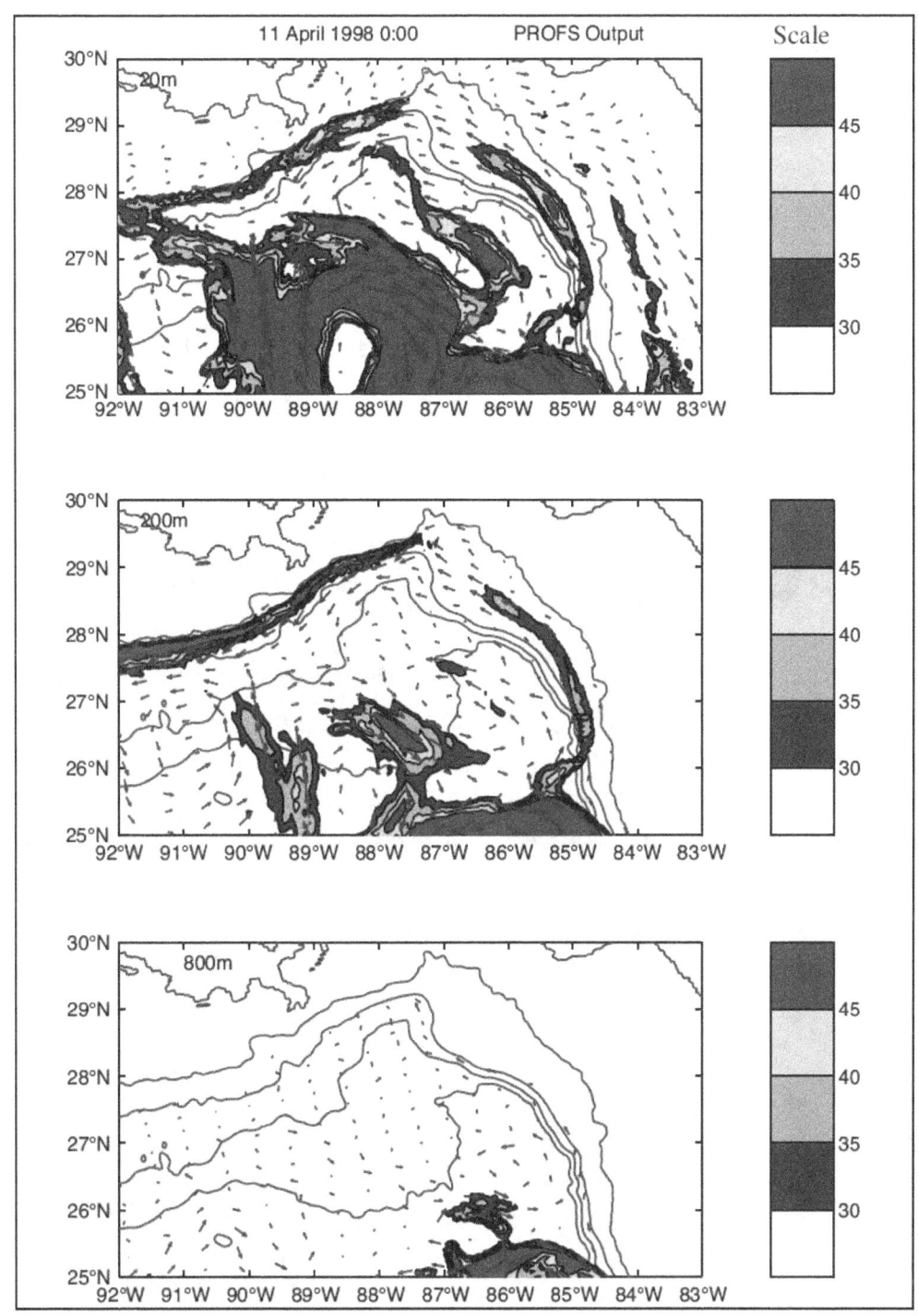

Figure 4.2-4. Contours and vectors of current speed from FGS PROFS model on 11 April 1998. Jet GC236 was also observed in the north-central Gulf of Mexico on this date. Panels are for depth level: 20 m (top), 200 m (middle), and 800 m (bottom). Red signifies currents in excess of 45 cm·s[1]. Figure courtesy Leo Oey (Princeton University).

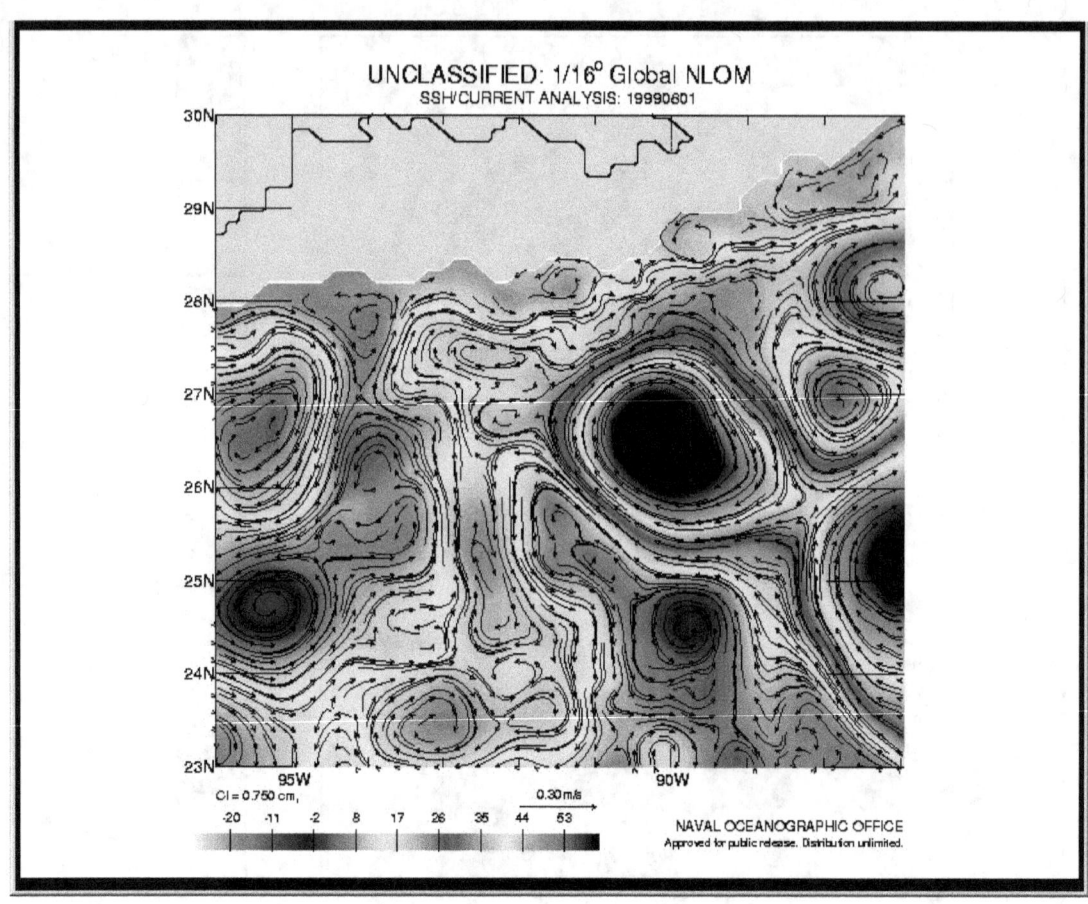

Figure 4.3-1. Sea-surface height field of north-central Gulf of Mexico from 1/16° Global NLOM model on 1 August 1999. Contour interval is 0.75 cm. (Figure courtesy T. Townsend of Naval Research Laboratory)

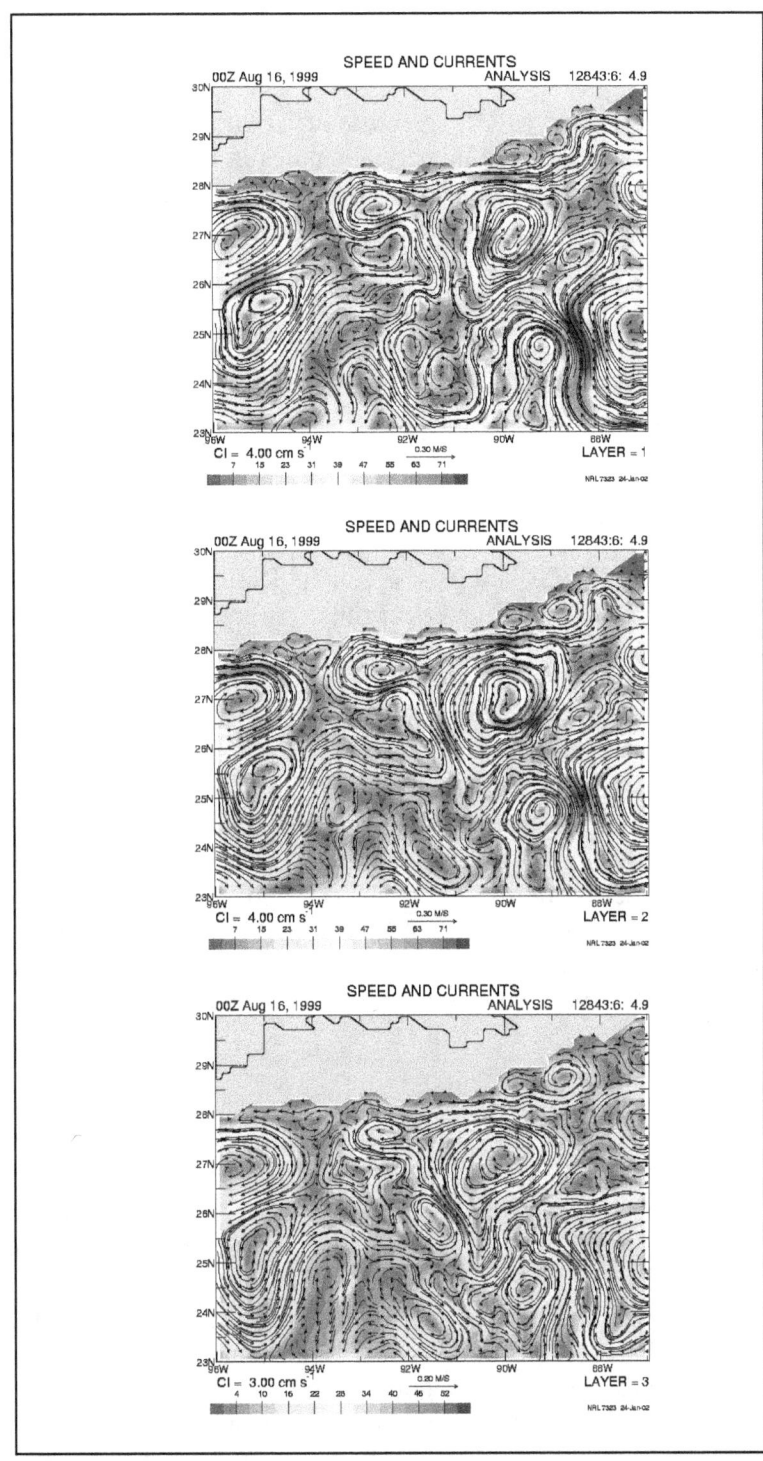

Figure 4.3-2. Current vectors and speed contours from 1/16° Global NLOM on 16 August 1999 from three model layer depths: 80 (top), 400 (middle), and 600 (bottom) m. Depth values are mean depths for layer. Contour interval for top and middle panel is 4 cm·s⁻¹; bottom panel contour interval is 3 cm·s⁻¹. (Figure is courtesy T. Townsend Naval Research Laboratory.)

4.4 AEF Analysis

Under the direction of the MMS and MRB, scientists at Accurate Environmental Forecasting, Inc., (AEF) performed a series of targeted numerical studies in an effort to determine possible generation mechanisms for sub-surface jets. The following section draws heavily from the results of AEF's analyses reported to MMS in April 2002 (Frolov et al., 2002). Two mechanisms for jet generation were investigated: violent interaction of preexisting small-scale eddies with rough topography and baroclinic instability in large-scale eddies.

4.4.1   Topographic Interaction

This inquiry sought to answer the question of whether sub-surface jets can be generated during the violent interaction of small-scale cyclones and/or LCEs with rough topography within the hydrostatic framework.

The general numerical experimental setup is given in Rothstein et al. (2003). Here, we concentrate only on those aspects of the numerical runs that are directly relevant to subsurface jets. A small cyclone (~100 km in diameter) is initialized next to a larger anticyclone (~350 km in diameter) over the continental slope of the northern Gulf of Mexico. The eddy centers are initially 200 km apart; the cyclonic eddy is west of the anticyclone.

Figure 4.4.1-1 shows the simulated temperature and velocity fields at 260 m after a month of model integration. The cyclone is seen squeezed between the anticyclone and the northern shelf. A second cyclone was generated northeast of the anticyclone by the advection of potential vorticity off the continental shelf (Rothstein et al. 2003). Soon after, the small cyclone moved eastward and merged with the second cyclone. The cyclone decreased in intensity most likely due to radiation of long gravity waves. There is no indication of significant current amplification at mid-water depths during the interaction. Therefore, this mechanism is thought to be an unlikely cause of subsurface jets.

4.4.2   Baroclinic Instability

The second investigation tried to identify mesoscale features that can be baroclinically unstable over a sloping bottom and to determine whether those features can produce jet-like disturbances. Two frontal structures that are baroclinically unstable over the bottom were identified; the structures correspond to two different scenarios of jet generation. The first scenario has an initial surface-intensified profile and corresponds to upper ocean kinetic energy being transferred to an intermediate depth layer. The second scenario is when kinetic energy confined to an intermediate layer is redistributed and focused into high-intensity jets via the sharpening of initially broad fronts. These two structures were then optimized to produce the most intense and fastest growing baroclinic instabilities. These optimized structures were then used to initialize eddy fields in a multilayer intermediate equation numerical model of the northern Gulf of Mexico (see Rothstein et al. 2003, for details).

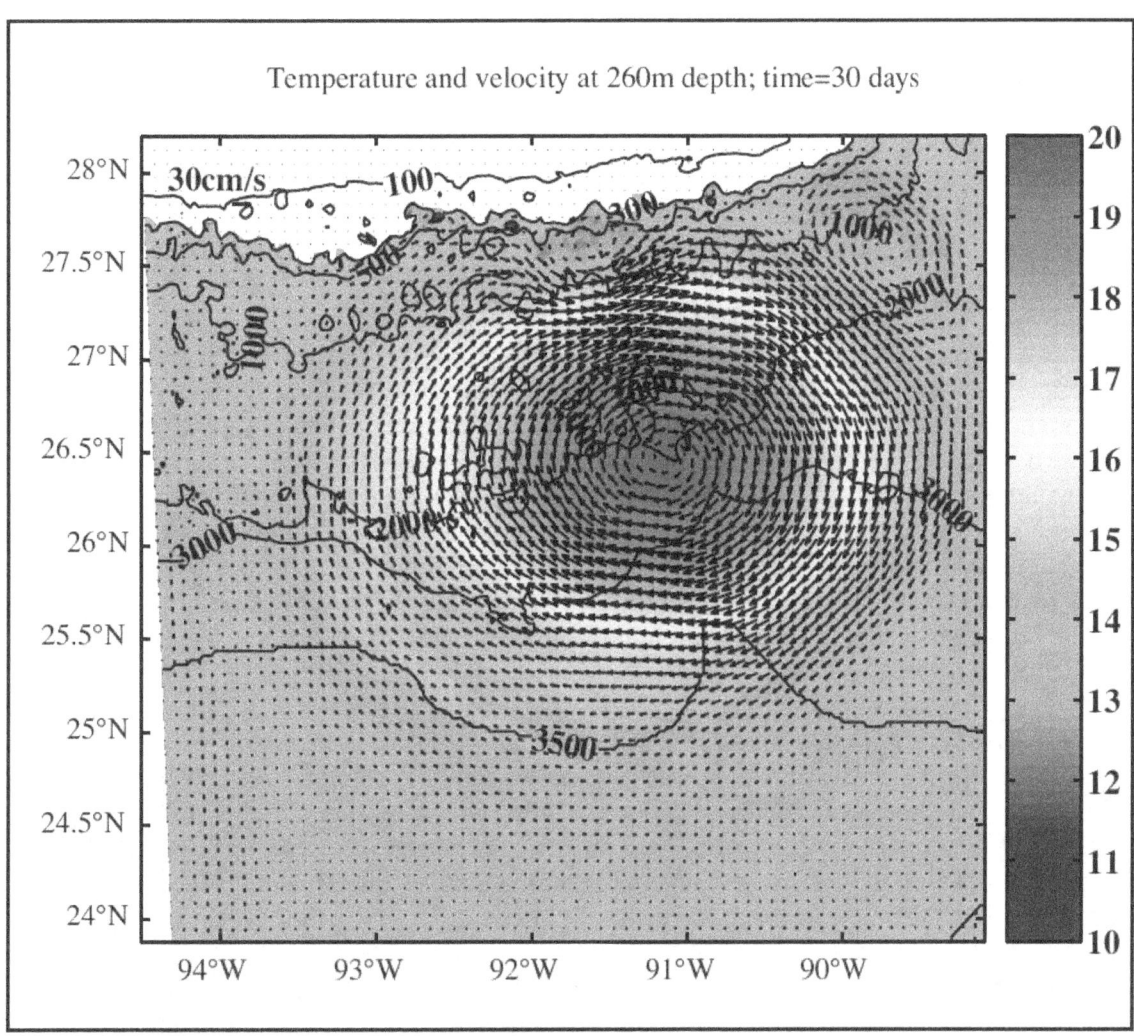

Figure 4.4.1-1 Simulation of a cyclone being squeezed between an LCE and topography. Shown are the simulated temperature and velocity fields at 260 m depth after one month of integration; the center of the cyclone is located approximately at 91.7°W, 27.6°N. Figure is courtesy of Accurate Environmental Forecasting, Inc.

The unstable surface-intensified frontal cross-section (first scenario) is shown in Figure 4.4.2-1 (upper). The necessary condition for baroclinic instability was satisfied due to the potential vorticity gradient inversion between the second and fourth layers with average (unperturbed) depths of 30 and 120 m, respectively. The maximum current speed reached 100 cm·s^{-1} near the surface (in the upper layer). The characteristic front width was 100 km, and the characteristic vertical scale was less than 200 m. The exponential growth rate for a zonal front with this structure was about 5 days; the wavelength of the most unstable wave (spatial scale of the instability) was 130 km.

The structure was used to construct an anticyclone with radius of 150 km. The shape of the anticyclone was slightly perturbed to create an initial disturbance that evolves into a series of undulations along the anticyclonic boundary. These undulations eventually pinch off and form small anticyclones. Figure 4.4.2-1 (lower) shows the fully nonlinear stage of PV and velocity field evolution in the mid-water column (170-350 m layer) after 30 days of model integration. The undulations along the anticyclone boundary cause stretching and squashing of the intermediate layer. This resulted in the generation of cyclonic and anticyclonic vortices. The currents in the intermediate layer reached a peak intensity of 20 cm·s^{-1} within the cyclonic vortices. The characteristic spatial scale of those currents was about 100 km with time scales of the order of 10 days.

The frontal structure for the unstable mid-water intensified case is shown in Figure 4.4.2-2 (upper). Here the instability condition was satisfied by the PV gradient inversion at model layers at the average (unperturbed) depths of 280 and 525 m. The maximum currents reached 40 cm·s^{-1} at 110 m. The characteristic front width was 60 km, and the characteristic vertical scale was 400 km. The exponential growth rate for a zonal front containing this structure was about 10 days; the wavelength of the most unstable wave was ~120 km.

The mid-water intensified structure (second scenario) was used to initialize a cyclone with 50 km radius. Figure 4.4.2-2 (lower) shows the PV and velocity field in the mid-water column (170-350 m) after 60 days of integration. Here, three smaller cyclones have formed. The mid-water currents intensified by 5 cm·s^{-1} reaching 45 cm·s^{-1}. The spatial and temporal scales of these currents are 50 km and ~20 days, respectively.

Based on these idealized numerical investigations, we have concluded that baroclinically unstable frontal structures are not particularly adept at producing currents that resemble the observed jet candidates. The simulated current jets typically are weaker in amplitude, have larger spatial scale, and long temporal scale. This is consistent with the findings from the full Gulf of Mexico realistic circulation models. However, this numerical exercise does substantiate that baroclinic instability is capable of channeling kinetic energy into the middle layers, therefore, this mechanism is still very likely to play an important role in generating/maintaining jets.

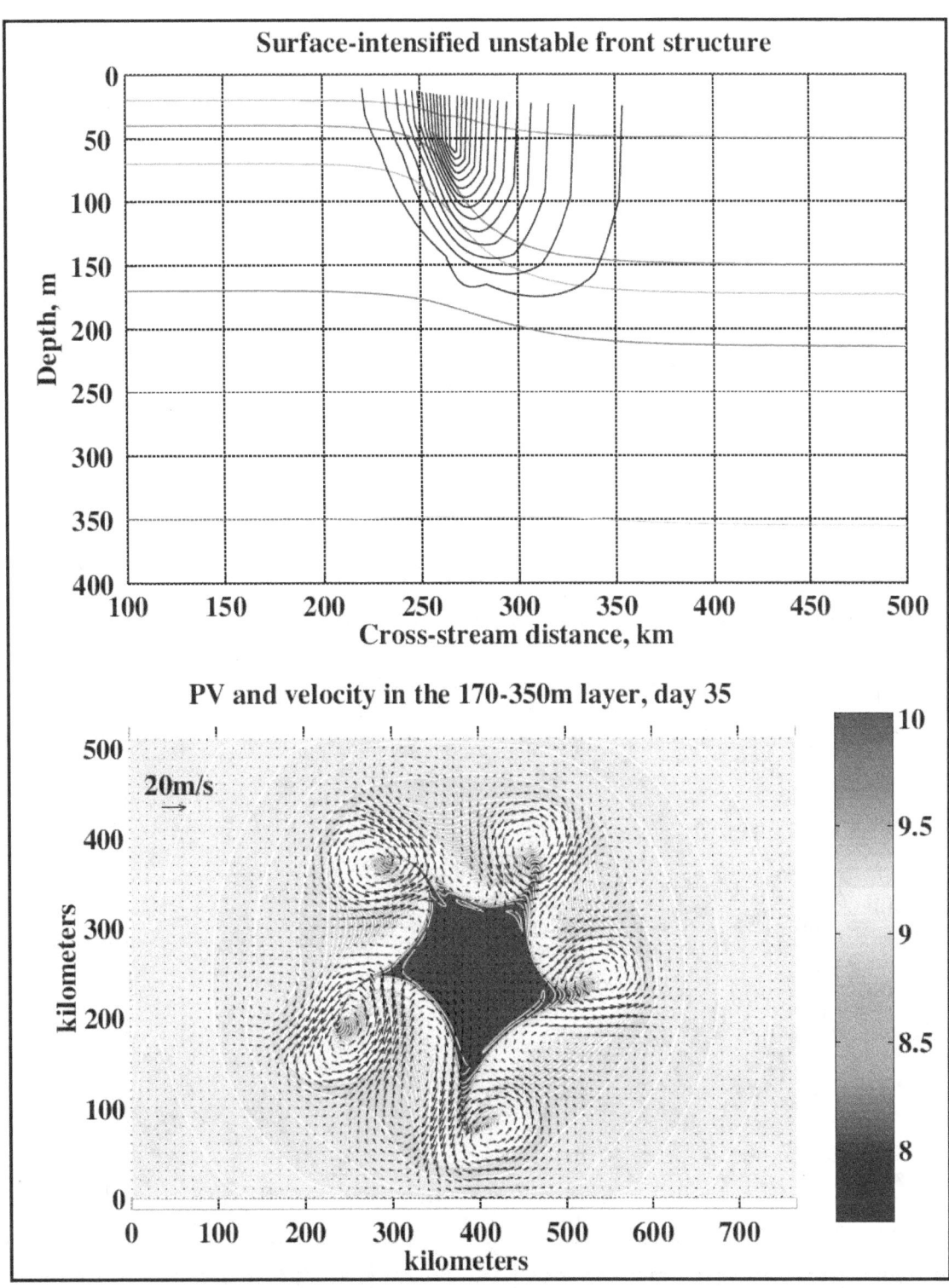

Figure 4.4.2-1. Unstable surface-intensified frontal structure (top) and the potential vorticity and velocity fields in the midwater column (170-350 m layer) after 30 days of model integration (bottom). Figure is courtesy of Accurate Environmental Forecasting, Inc.

81

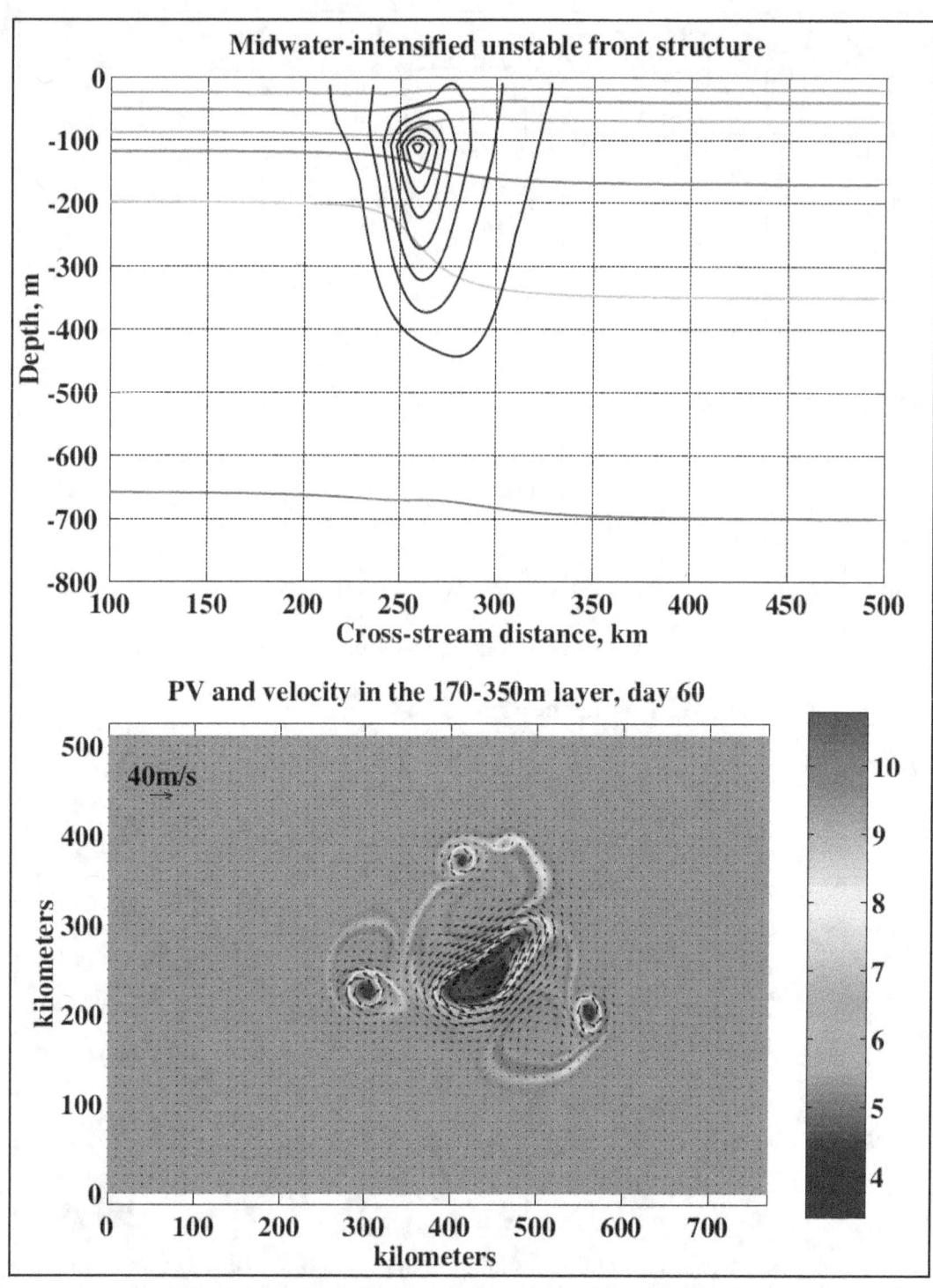

Figure 4.4.2-2. Unstable mid-depth-intensified frontal structure (top) and potential vorticity and velocity fields in the midcolumn (170-350 m layer) after 60 days of integration (bottom). Figure courtesy of Accurate Environmental Forecasting, Inc.

5. MECHANISMS

Identifying and testing the mechanisms responsible for jet generation was limited by a number of factors. The small number of jet candidates found in the observations did not allow for meaningful statistical measures of jet events beyond basic estimates of duration, speed, and vertical extent. The lack of any vertical measures of temperature or salinity made any verifiable conclusions of baroclinic mechanisms speculative. The fact that all were measured from singly locations precluded estimations of horizontal scales. Additionally, instrumentation and deployment issues complicated the interpretation of several of the candidates.

Mechanism testing using numerical model outputs was also of limited use. Although the numerical models available for use in this study were state of the art, there remain lingering questions whether the horizontal resolution (in some cases 3-5 km) was adequate to resolve the small-scale structures likely to be associated with jet events. Further, the indication of inhomogeneous flow as measured by the long-range ADCPs challenges the view that the hydrostatic formulation of these numerical models is appropriate on features with time scales as short as a several hours to a couple of days.

However, we have speculated on a number of candidate causal mechanisms of the jet generation. Some candidate mechanisms seem more likely than others. Examples of unlikely candidates: buoyant coastal fronts (the jets are too far from shore and river plumes), upwelling (peak speeds are slower in upwelling which usually are essentially surface intensified), and under-currents (no evidence such a current exists in the Gulf of Mexico. The more likely candidates include: (a) baroclinic instability, (b) motions derived from Loop Current and associated eddies in the form of filaments and meanders, (c) motions due to ring/ring and/or slope-shelf/ring interaction, (d) reversed baroclinicity (Onken 1990), or (e) manifestations of internal waves with unusually large speeds. The latter could result from superposition of internal wave trains, i.e. rogue internal waves, superposition on low-frequency motions, or intensification in regions of enhanced shear.

The remainder of this section discusses those mechanisms that seem to have potential to account for jet events. The mechanisms are divided into two groups: plausible and possible (yet unlikely).

5.1 Summary of Plausible Physical Mechanisms

5.1.1 Baroclinic Instability

The mechanism of baroclinic instability would seem to be the most plausible physical mechanism responsible for jet generation. The Frontal Air-Sea Interaction Experiment (FASINEX) conducted southwest of Bermuda in the mid-1980s was designed to investigate air-sea interaction on 1-100 km horizontal scales near strong horizontal upper ocean gradients (Weller 1991). An unexpected finding of this experiment was the discovery of sub-frontal scale cold-core features (horizontal scale of 15-25 km) that could result from instabilities of the baroclinic front (Weller and Samelson 1991).

Several observational and theoretical investigations of the evolution of baroclinic instabilities soon followed. Notable are the numerical investigations of Samelson (1993) and Samelson and

Chapman (1995). Samelson (1993) focuses on the linear instability problem, while Samelson and Chapman (1995) extend the investigation to a fully nonlinear evolution of the frontal instability and the formation of cold-core eddies along a geostrophically balanced mixed-layer front. Samelson and Chapman (1995) report there are large horizontal and vertical heat and potential vorticity fluxes associated with the evolution of instability. Computed maximum vertical velocities associated with the fastest growing instability mode reach 2.5×10^{-2} cm·s^{-1}. Heat fluxes are confined above the thermocline, however, potential vorticity fluxes are maximum 50-75 m deeper and extend into the thermocline to about 250 m. This numerically computed mode leads to cold-core features that are consistent with the FASINEX cold-core eddy observations. The selective formation of small-scale cold-core features is also confirmed in the numerical investigations presented in Section 4.4. The large vertical velocities (and implied large vertical accelerations) suggest that a nonhydrostatic framework would be more appropriate for further numerical investigation into this mechanism.

Unfortunately, the FASINEX studies were confined mostly to the mixed-layer and upper thermocline (i.e., between 50 and 150 m). But as was seen in Section 4.4, baroclinic instability can be an effective way to channel kinetic energy into water depths deeper than 150 m.

An indication of the evolution of a cold core feature along the frontal boundary of a Loop Current Eddy in the northern Gulf of Mexico occurred in spring of 2001. During 16 April 2001, the newly detached Millennium Eddy moved northward over the north-central slope of the Gulf of Mexico. As the northern limb of this eddy interacted with the continental slope, the frontal boundary became aligned with the east-west bathymetry of the shelf break. By 18 April 2003, the northern boundary of the eddy showed a depression pushing in toward the center of the eddy. This was evidenced in sea surface temperature fields from AVHRR satellite. By 26 April, the depression had evolved into a cyclonic swirl roughly 50 km in diameter. Figure 5.1.1-1 shows the sea surface height of the Gulf of Mexico based on altimetry on 26 April 2001. The eddy with diameter about 300-km is seen centered near 26.5°N, 90°W. The cyclonic eddy is not visible in this image due to the horizontal resolution of the altimeter and the temporal averaging used to produce the plot. However, in the three-day composite sea surface temperature field based on AVHRR satellite imagery, the cold eddy is identified near 28°N, 89.5°W on the northeast limb of the eddy (Figure 5.1.1-2). Further evidence of the cyclonic rotation is provided by near surface drifting buoys seeded into the eddy. Eventually, the cold eddy grows in size and strength and moves clockwise on the periphery of Millennium Eddy.

Current observations by industry in the vicinity of the cold eddy (not shown) suggest the presence of a subsurface jet. The EW913 jet event may also be linked with this mechanism as Eddy Juggernaut impinged on the northern slope in August 1999. Sea surface temperature during that month also indicates a frontal eddy between the slope and Eddy Juggernaut. The jet events in lease blocks VK956, GC505a, MC628, GC236, and GC506 are all associated with LCE frontal boundaries or small scale cold core cyclones.

The dynamics of small-scale features found along the periphery of the Loop Current and Loop Current Eddies is currently a topic of intense research. This is possible mainly due to increased

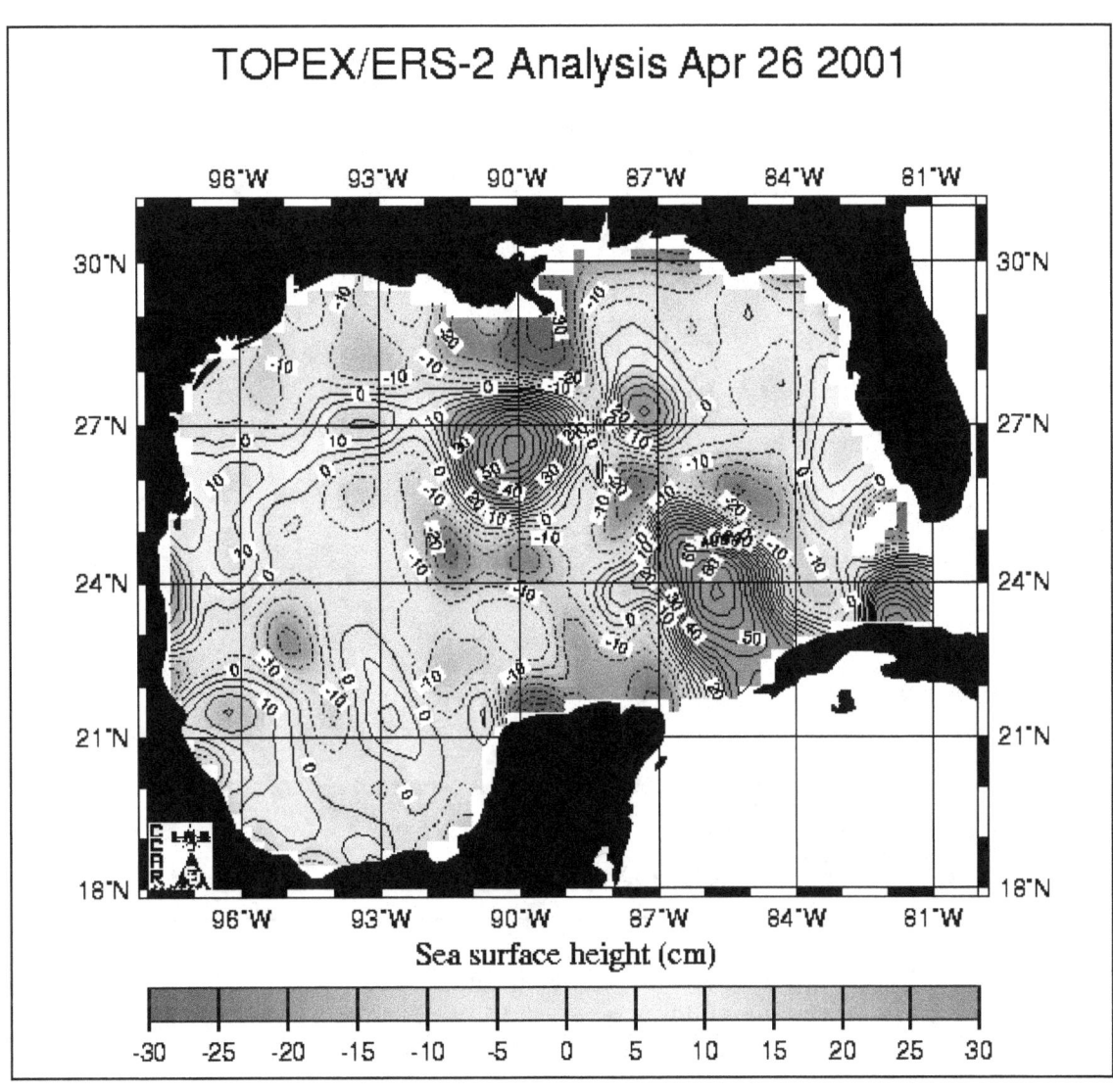

Figure 5.1.1-1. Sea-surface height of the Gulf of Mexico from satellite altimeter data for 26 April 2001. Millennium Eddy is centered near 90°W, 26.5°N.

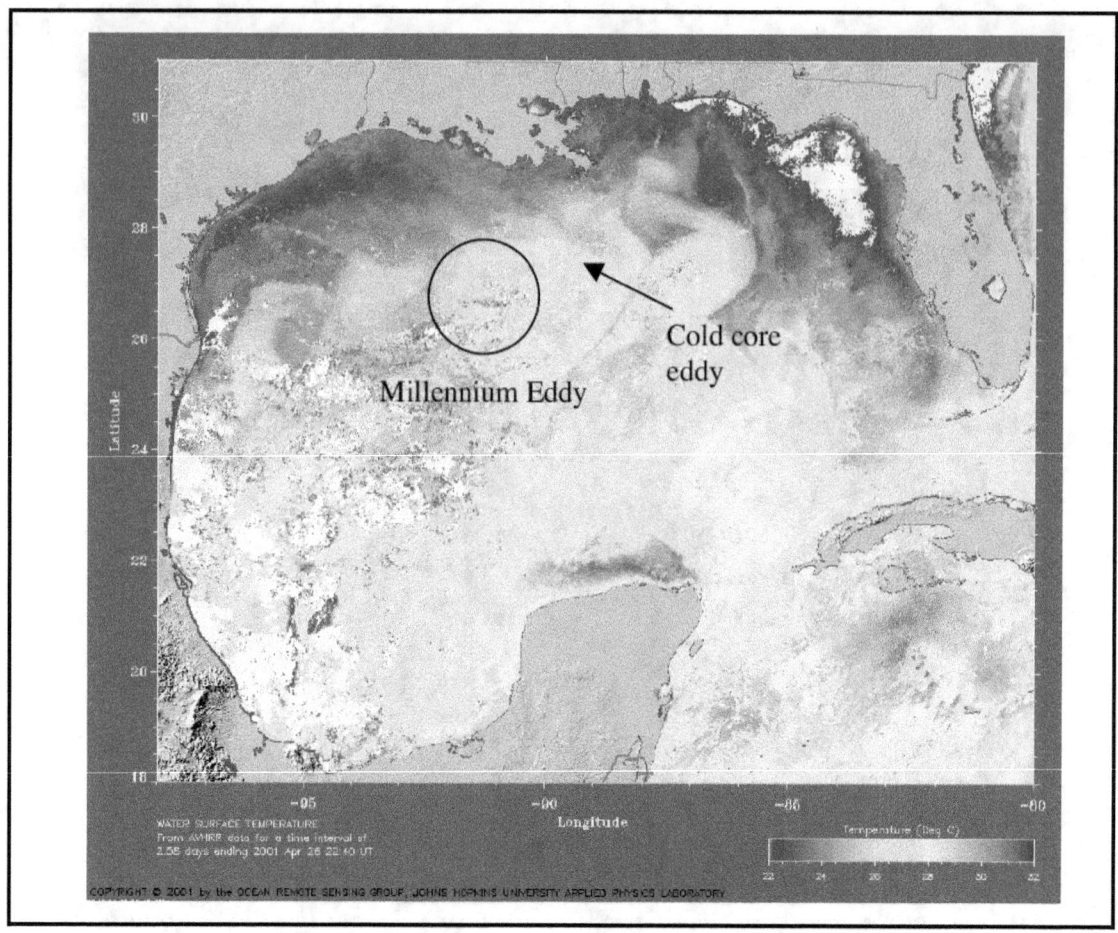

Figure 5.1.1-2. AVHRR image of sea-surface temperature of the Gulf of Mexico on 26 April 2001. Millennium Eddy is seen near 90°W, 26.5°N; a smaller cold core eddy has formed northeast of the larger Millennium Eddy. Image is courtesy of Johns Hopkins Applied Physics Laboratory.

horizontal resolution of satellite imagery and numerical models. Some have suggested that frontal (or parasitic) eddies are directly linked to Loop Current separation and Loop Current Eddy decay.

5.1.2   Inertial Wave Train

Though technically not a jet, the downward propagation of inertial oscillations should certainly be considered a mechanism that can explain some subsurface jet-like events. Evidence for this is clearly seen in the DC277 record (Section 3.1.9) caused by Hurricane Georges in September 1998. However, the inertial wave train does not have to be limited to the downward propagation of storm-generated currents. Inertial oscillations are ubiquitous in the ocean and can be initiated by many forcing mechanisms including eddies. Full water column current meter measurements made in 2000 m depth off the Sigsbee Escarpment in the Gulf of Mexico near 90°W show inertial and super-inertial kinetic energy increases in the presence of a Loop Current Eddy or the

86

Loop Current. Further, the superposition of an inertial wave packet on a filament of the Loop Current or LCE can cause a short-lived increase in speed which can make an otherwise weak current temporarily satisfy the criteria associated with a jet.

5.1.3 Reversed Baroclinicity

The phenomena of reversed baroclinicity as described by Onken (1990) explains the occurrence of the maximum submerged azimuthal flow occurring near 100 m in energetic eddies as due to kinematics that creates a thermostad, i.e., a layer of uniform temperature, in the upper 200 m of an eddy. Onken states only models with very good vertical resolution will be capable of realizing this effect. Unfortunately, the CUPOM and PROFS output available to this study is not adequately resolved for this purpose. A schematic of the effect taken from Onken (1990) is presented as Figure 5.1.3-1. Here the top figure can be considered to represent a radial section through a anticyclonic eddy. Figure 5.1.3-1b shows a similar section through a cyclonic eddy. A thermostad is seen centered between the seasonal and main thermocline at about 100 m depth in Figure 5.1.3-1a. Thick lines represent isotachs of velocity in increments of 10 cm·s^{-1} with submerged current maxima occurring roughly 70 km from the eddy center.

5.1.4 Filaments of Loop Current or Loop Current Eddy

Isolated submerged filaments or squirts of the Loop Current or Loop Current Eddy were frequently encountered in the numerical output available to this study. The strongest filaments and squirts usually occurred when a circulation was established along steep bathymetry along the upper slope. The filaments tended to be non-stationary and meander. It is possible that such an event has been captured in one or more of the jet observations as a filament meandered over and away from a current meter. However, this would be impossible to prove given the limited spatial coverage of the measurements during any of the observed jets.

5.2 Summary of Possible (But Unlikely) Physical Mechanisms

5.2.1 Internal Solitary Waves

Internal solitons (a sequence of internal solitary waves) of very large amplitude can occur in the ocean, and can be associated with large velocity. The most striking examples are those observed n the Andaman Sea (Osborne and Burch, 1980). These occurred in a depth of about 160 m below the surface and the lead solitary wave had a vertical scale of about 60 m and a time scale of about 30 minutes between successive peaks (Osborne et al., 1983). The mechanism that produced these waves was interaction of the barotropic tide with a strait sill. While this mechanism is not likely in the Gulf of Mexico, another likely mechanism is by disintegration of internal tides due to breaking when they propagate across the continental slope. Figure 5.2.1-1 is a schematic cross section of an internal soliton in a two-layer fluid taken from Osborne and Burch (1980). Dashed lines represent constant current speed with arrows indicating current direction and magnitude. The soliton is formed as a wave around a propagating depression in the interface between fluids of different density. Note the large vertical velocities proceeding and following the depression.

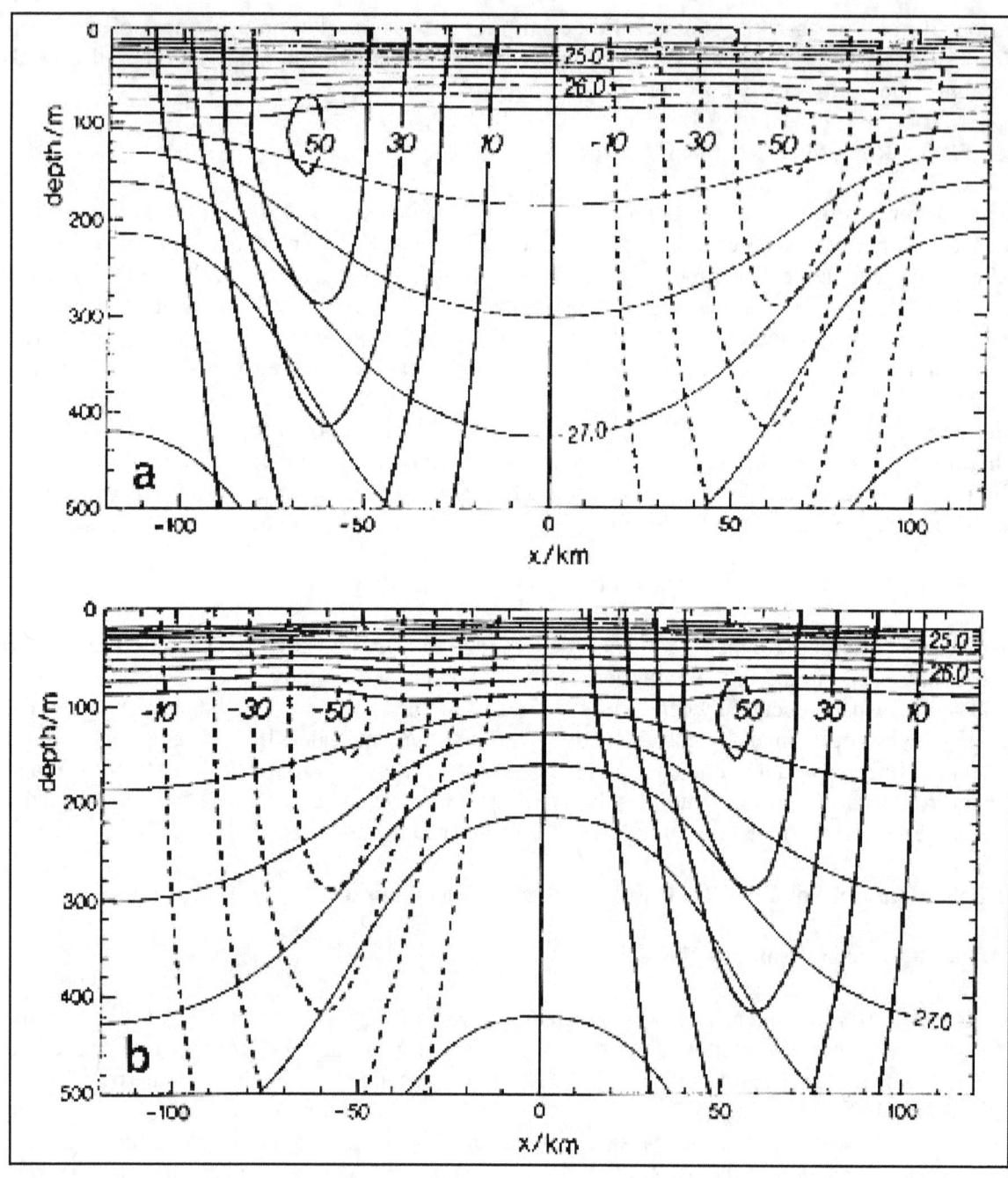

Figure 5.1.3-1. Radial sections through (a) an anticyclone and (b) a cyclone. These lines are σ_t surfaces in increments of 0.1 kg·m^{-3}. Thick lines are isotachs of azimuthal velocity in increments of 10 cm·s^{-1}. Taken from Onken (1990).

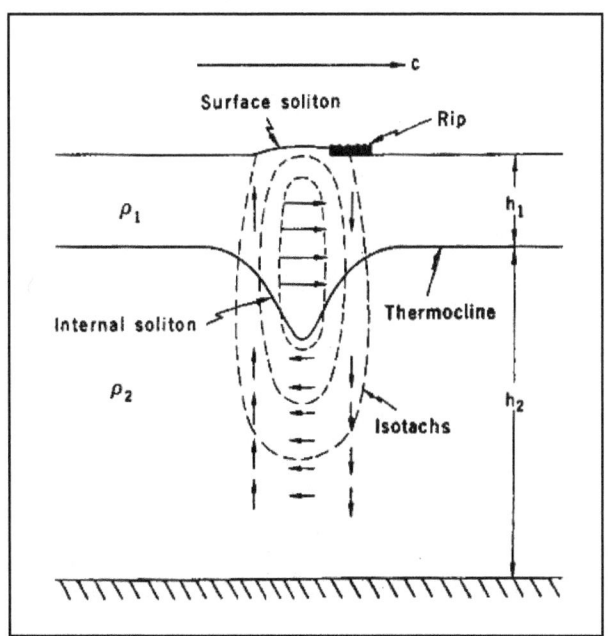

Figure 5.2.1-1. Internal soliton in a two-layer fluid of finite depth. The depression of the interface can propagate when $h_1 < h_2$. Dashed lines are isotachs; arrows indicate magnitude and direction of flow. A small surface soliton (rip) accompanies the internal soliton. Taken from Osborne and Burch (1980).

89

Internal solitons occurring in the Adaman Sea had maximum horizontal velocities (55 cm·s^{-1}) at around 87-m depth and had surface rip bands proceeding the soliton arrival. The duration of these internal solitons was about 17 minutes.

Vlasenko (1994) derived a general analytical solution for an internal solitary wave through the use of multiple vertical modes. The first baroclinic mode has been used to describe the observed solitary waves. However, in theory the higher vertical modes exist and are mid-depth intensified. Thus, the jets of the Gulf of Mexico have the potential to be explained as trains of high-order internal solitary waves initiated by strong current-topographic interaction. A nonhydrostatic model is needed to verify this.

5.2.2   Flow Over Undulating Bottom

The effects of deep flow over an undulating seas bed can cause downward and upward flux of kinetic energy in the water column at relatively high frequency (Rhines 1977). Such effects may cause the production of submerged jets in much the same way as strong winds in the vicinity of mountains and hills can produce mountain waves (Gill 1982). However, there is no evidence as to whether the density structure in the Gulf of Mexico can support this generation mechanism and achieve current with the amplitudes seen in the observations.

5.3 Additional Annotated References Possibly Relevant to Submerged Jets

Beckmann, A., 1988. Vertical structure of mid-latitude mesoscale instabilities, *J. Phys. Oceanogr.*, **18**, 1354-1371. This paper addresses stable and unstable vertical modes of low frequency perturbations in a stratified fluid with vertical shear of the basic flow. These modes can have maximum disturbances at subsurface levels for disturbances that are of small horizontal scale (order 40 km). The paper is perhaps more pertinent to the instability of an existing current system, like the Loop Current or Gulf Stream.

Howden, S. D. and D. R. Watts, 1999. Jet streaks in the Gulf Stream, *J. Phys. Oceanogr.*, **29**, 1910-1924. The authors draw an analogy between the jet streaks in the Gulf Stream and those studied in the atmospheric jet stream. These streaks can be regarded as a superposition of the basic baroclinic stream and a barotropic eddy that leads to localized maxima in speed that propagates relative to the main stream. Such features are seen at several levels (400, 700, and 1000 m).

LaCasce, J. H., 1998. A geostrophic vortex over a slope, *J. Phys. Oceanogr.*, 28, 2362- 2381. This is a very definitive extension of the earlier study by Smith and O'Brien (1983) on the dynamics of eddies interacting with topography in the context of a two layer system. The paper focuses on the evolution of initially barotropic and initially surface trapped eddies. Patterns of potential vorticity as well as stream function are employed to illustrate the evolutionary stages of eddies. The fragmentation of the lower layer structure in some cases may be relevant to the kind of disturbances that industry has identified as subsurface jets.

Munk. W., 1981. Internal waves and small-scale processes, in **Evolution of Physical Oceanography**, B. Warren and C. Wunsch, Editors, The MIT Press, 164-191. Munk includes a discussion of the behavior of internal wave packets near a critical layer in a stably stratified fluid in the presence of vertical shear of the mean current.

Olbers, D. K., 1981. The propagation of internal waves in a Geostrophic current, *J. Phys. Oceanogr.*, **11**, 1224-1233. This paper addresses the influence of the ambient velocity shear on the propagation and possible amplification of the high frequency currents associated with internal wave packets at critical layers in the fluid.

Smith, D. C., IV, and J. J. O'Brien, 1983. The interaction of a two-layer isolated mesoscale eddy with bottom topography, *J. Phys. Oceanogr.*, **13**, 1681-1697. The authors employ a non-linear two-layer model to address the interaction of a westward propagating eddy with a western continental slope. The non-linearity tends to hold the eddy together over the slope.

Vallis, G. K. and M. E. Maltrud, 1993. Generation of mean flows and jets on a beta plane and over topography, *J. Phys. Oceanogr.*, **23**, 1346-1362. This is a very informative paper on the implications of the conservation of potential vorticity about mean flow over topography. It is most pertinent to the case in which mean cyclonic circulation is seen along the lateral boundaries beneath anticyclonic circulation of the upper waters. The mechanism is the same as that which causes deep poleward flow in ocean basins beneath eastern boundary currents and equatorward flow beneath western boundary currents. The deep mean flow represents bottom trapped current.

6. MEASUREMENT RECOMMENDATIONS

6.1 General Recommendations for Measurements on Offshore Platforms

In response to the MMS request for "guidance on how to collect data on drill and production platforms" in the northern Gulf of Mexico we offered the recommendations to follow. The objective of these measurements would be to obtain accurate near real-time profiles of speed and direction from platforms in the Gulf of Mexico. These data could support many uses including model assimilation and emerging observing systems.

1. Future deployments of ADCPs on fixed platforms should be 38 kHz instruments, e.g., RDI 38 kHz Ocean Observer, which feature an advertised penetration of 730 to 1000+ m with cell sizes of 16 to 24 m. Standard sensors include tilt, temperature, and a fluxgate compass. The instrument should be mounted in a fixed bracket and away from structures and well below the wave zone. A fluxgate compass is affected by nearby iron so the ADCP should be located below the principal component of the platform by at least 20 m. Mounting below the rig also avoids interference between the acoustic beams and the structure.

2. Temperature and salinity profiles and meteorological information also would be useful for a variety of studies, but the two former are likely of less value than winds and certainly less than currents.

3. Deep current measurements. Not necessarily feasible on drilling platforms, deep current measurements would be desirable on fixed platforms, particularly if instruments can be easily maintained and do not interfere with service vessels, work activities, etc. Instrumentation should be single-point current meters or ADCPs of appropriate frequency depending upon the expected size of scatterers present. Also T-S recorders should be considered in special cases. The instrument system should be installed so it will not interfere with, and be somewhat protected, from production activities. The effects of the platform itself on the currents also should be considered when determining instrument placement.

4. Simplicity of measurement system. The platform-based data acquisition system must be kept as simple as possible to avoid being unnecessarily complex and must be configured to run largely unattended once set up.

5. Backups/archival. The on-board data logging system should consist of a dedicated PC-type system with a tape backup mechanism and copious amounts of hard disk capacity to accommodate the deployment and minimize workload during backup to tape. Backups should be regularly sent to an onshore facility for further processing, gap filling, and long-term archival. The importance of system monitoring, maintenance, backups, and delivery of backups to shore cannot be overemphasized and must be communicated to rig operators by their management to ensure data integrity.

6. Telemetry and central onshore facility. Data recorded offshore should be telemetered to a central facility where QA/QC and redistribution will take place. All data should be examined, archived, and distributed as required by a single group experienced in such work. Data

should be accessed for quality, appropriate metadata added, and quality ranking assigned. Multiple records at a single location should be aggregated into longer time series. Basic statistical products should be prepared and distributed. A catalog of collected data together with appropriate derived quantities should be developed and maintained on a user-friendly web site.

6.2 Specific Recommendations for Jets

In addition to the general recommendations regarding routine data collection on platforms we present the following recommendations that are specific to data collection strategies capable of capturing a jet event.

1. Moored time series measurements. Locations where jet candidates are known to have occurred (i.e., the slope regions of the north-central Gulf of Mexico) should be instrumented with ADCPs. The deployments should be long-term (order of years), have at least hourly temporal resolution, and cover the upper 500 m of the water column with a maximum bin size of 20 m. The instrumentation should be as isolated as possible from drilling and production operation. Since the density structure of the water column is completely unknown during any jet event thus far observed, it is imperative to measure salinity and temperature as well as current velocity at multiple depths. Multiple sites would increase the probability of encountering a jet and could produce desperately needed data on jet scales and extent.

    A moored measurement program specifically designed to capture shelf edge filaments would require two to three closely spaced cross-shelf mooring lines near 91°W. The MMS-funded Eddy Intrusion Study was not suitable (or designed) to detect this type of structure because few current measurements were taken in depths between 100 and 500 m below the surface. The proposed measurement program would require 75 kHz ADCPs to sample the depth range from the surface to 500 m. These measurements should be supplemented with thermistor/conductivity strings to provide much needed density observations.

2. XBT deployments from platforms. The most unknown aspect of the jets so far encountered is the density structure. To our knowledge, the only density information available during a jet event are temperatures recorded by ADCP, which are measured at the transducer head and remote from the jet core, and AVHRR sea surface temperature fields also remote from the jet core. Neither transducer temperature nor SST fields are sufficient to estimate a density profile during a jet. If XBTs were launched from manned platforms at the onset of a jet event and continued at regular time intervals during and after the event, then many possible mechanisms could be included or excluded.

3. Ship survey. Quasi-synoptic ship surveys might be made during jet events. At a minimum, survey ships should be outfitted with standard hydrographic instrumentation (CTD, XBT, etc.) and 75 kHz shipboard ADCPs capable of reaching 500 m depth. Surveys could be supplemented with tracer experiments, surface drifters, and sub-surface floats. The difficulty, of course, is that vessels are unlikely to be on site at the time of occurrences of jets. Several different measurement strategies could be instituted during the surveys. For example, satellite imagery could reveal the presence of a developing cyclone on the upper slope in response to

eddy-slope interaction. A hydrographic survey of the region could then commence to detect the presence of baroclinic instability along the eddy frontal boundary. Shipboard ADCP could provide current profiles and detect the presence of jets. The satellite imagery could be used to help adapt the sampling scheme to account for real-time changes in the features being sampled. This would require rapid outfitting and mobilization of a ship after the feature is detected. However, given that the baroclinic instabilities presumed from SST images of the Gulf of Mexico tend to develop over periods ranging from a few weeks to a couple months, there is time to properly outfit a research vessel capable of carrying the necessary equipment and instrumentation and to design an adequate survey plan capable of capturing the instability.

4. Collect acoustic profiler data in single ping mode. This would allow the analyst to identify the structure of the inhomogeneity rather than speculating from an averaged product. Collect data in beam coordinates. This would allow for the analysis of radial velocities before they are transformed into earth coordinates. Transform to earth coordinates during post-processing. Single ping radial velocities that are suspect can be eliminated and greatly improve overall data quality. A fifth transducer oriented along the instruments axis would provide a direct measure of the vertical velocity. This direct measurement could then be compared with the calculated vertical velocity from the other four beams and give an indication of the presence or absence of nonhomogeneous flow.

5. New modeling initiatives. MMS should continue their interest in numerical model investigations that include nonhydrostatic processes, i.e., DieCAST, as well as idealized numerical investigations of baroclinic instability and eddy-slope interaction. The idealized investigations should proceed in the manner that AEF conducted numerical experiments using hydrostatic models. The model dynamics would then evolves from prescribed Loop Current Eddies, cyclones, and other structures.

7. REFERENCES

Beckmann, A. 1988. Vertical structure of mid-latitude mesoscale instabilities. J. Phys. Oceanogr. 18:1354-1371.

Farrant, T. and K. Javed. 2001. Minimising the effect of deepwater currents on drilling riser operations. Deepwater Drilling Technologies, Aberdeen Marriot, Aberdeen. January 2001. 15 pp.

Frolov, S., G.D. Rowe, L.M. Rothstein, and I. Ginis. 2002. Cross-shelf exchange processes and the deep-water circulation of the Gulf of Mexico: the dynamical effects of submarine canyons and the interaction of Loop Current Eddies with topography. Quarterly Report No. 10. Accurate Environmental Forecasting, Inc. 19 pp.

Frolov, S.A., G.D. Rowe, L.M. Rothstein, and I. Ginis. In press. Cross-Shelf Exchange Processes and the Deepwater Circulation of the Gulf of Mexico: Dynamical Effects of Submarine Canyons and the Interactions of Loop Current Eddies with Topography. Final Report, U.S. Dept. of the Interior, Minerals Management Service, Gulf of Mexico OCS Region, New Orleans, LA.

Gill, A.E. 1982. Atmosphere-Ocean Dynamics. Volume 30, International Geophysics Series. New York: Academic Press. 662 pp.

Gordon, R.L. 1996. Acoustic Doppler Current Profilers, Principles of Operation: A Practical Primer. Second Edition for BroadBand ADCPs, San Diego: RD Instruments. 54 pp.

Howden, S.D. and D.R. Watts. 1999. Jet streaks in the Gulf Stream. J. Phys. Oceanogr. 29:1910-1924.

Jochens, A.E., S.F. DiMarco, W.D. Nowlin Jr., R.O. Reid, and M.C. Kennicutt II. 2002. Northeastern Gulf of Mexico Chemical Oceanography and Hydrography Study: Synthesis Report. U.S. Dept. of the Interior, Minerals Management Service, Gulf of Mexico OCS Region, New Orleans, LA. OCS Study MMS 2002-055. 586 pp.

Kantha, L., J.-K. Choi, R. Leben, C. Cooper, M. Vogel, and J. Feeney. 1999. Hindcasts and real-time nowcast/forecasts of currents in the Gulf of Mexico. Offshore Technology Conference (OTC 1999), May 3-6, 1999, Houston, Texas.

LaCasce, J.H. 1998. A geostrophic vortex over a slope. J. Phys. Oceanogr. 28:2362-2381.

Munk, W. 1981. Internal waves and small-scale processes. In: Warren, B. and C. Wunsch, eds. Evolution of Physical Oceanography. The MIT Press. Pp. 164-191.

Nowlin, W.D. Jr., A.E. Jochens, S.F. DiMarco, R.O. Reid, and M.K. Howard. 2001. Deepwater Physical Oceanography Reanalysis and Synthesis of Historical Data: Synthesis Report. U.S. Dept. of the Interior, Minerals Management Service, Gulf of Mexico OCS Region, New Orleans, LA. OCS Study 2001-064. 528 pp.

Nystrom, E.A., K.A. Oberg, and C.R. Rehmann. 2002. Measurements of turbulence with acoustic Doppler current profilers: sources of error and laboratory results. In: Wahl, T., K. Oberg, and C. Pugh, eds. Proceedings of the Hydraulic Measurements and Experimental Methods Conference, Estes Park, CO 2002. ASCE. 10 pp.

Oey, L.-Y., P. Hamilton, and H.C. Lee. In Press. Modeling and Data Analyses of Circulation Processes in the Gulf of Mexico. Final Report, U.S. Dept. of the Interior, Minerals Management Service, Gulf of Mexico OCS Region, New Orleans, LA.

Olbers, D.K. 1981. The propagation of internal waves in a Geostrophic current. J. Phys. Oceanogr. 11:1224-1233.

Onken, R. 1990. The creation of reversed baroclinicity and subsurface jets in oceanic eddies. J. Phys. Oceanogr. 20:786-791.

Osborne, A.R. and T.I. Burch. 1980. Internal solitons in the Andaman Sea. Science 208:451-460.

Osborne, A.R., A. Provenzale, and L. Bergamasco. 1983. The nonlinear Fourier analysis of internal solitons in the Andaman Sea. Lettere al Nuovo Cimento 36(18):593-599.

Rhines, P.B. 1977. The dynamics of unsteady currents. In: The Sea: Volume 6, Marine Modeling. New York: John Wiley & Sons. Pp. 189-318.

Samelson, R.M., and D.C. Chapman. 1995. Evolution of the instability of a mixed layer front. J. Geophys. Research 100(C4):6743-6759.

Samelson, R.M. 1993. Linear instability of a mixed layer front. J. Geophys. Research 98(C6):10195-10204.

Smith, D.C. IV and J.J. O'Brien. 1983. The interaction of a two-layer isolated mesoscale eddy with bottom topography. J. Phys. Oceanogr. 13:1681-1697.

Sturges, W., E. Chassignet, and T. Ezer. In press. Strong Mid-Depth Currents and a Deep Cyclonic Gyre in the Gulf of Mexico. Final Report. U.S. Dept. of the Interior, Minerals Management Service, Gulf of Mexico OCS Region, New Orleans, LA.

Weller, R. 1991. Overview of the Frontal Air-Sea Interaction Experiment (FASINEX): A study of air-sea interaction in a region of strong oceanographic gradients. J. Geophys. Research 96(C5):8501-8516.

Weller, R., and R. Samelson. 1991. Upper ocean variability associated with fronts. In Potter, J. and A. Warn-Varnas, eds. Ocean Variability and Acoustic Propagation. Hingham, MA: Kluwar Academic. Pp. 463-478.

Vallis, G.K. and M.E. Maltrud. 1993. Generation of mean flows and jets on a beta plane and over topography. J. Phys. Oceanogr. 23:1346-1362.

Vlasenko, V. 1994. Multi-modal solition of internal waves. Atmos. Oceanic Phys. 30:161-169.

The Department of the Interior Mission

As the Nation's principal conservation agency, the Department of the Interior has responsibility for most of our nationally owned public lands and natural resources. This includes fostering sound use of our land and water resources; protecting our fish, wildlife, and biological diversity; preserving the environmental and cultural values of our national parks and historical places; and providing for the enjoyment of life through outdoor recreation. The Department assesses our energy and mineral resources and works to ensure that their development is in the best interests of all our people by encouraging stewardship and citizen participation in their care. The Department also has a major responsibility for American Indian reservation communities and for people who live in island territories under U.S. administration.

The Minerals Management Service Mission

As a bureau of the Department of the Interior, the Minerals Management Service's (MMS) primary responsibilities are to manage the mineral resources located on the Nation's Outer Continental Shelf (OCS), collect revenue from the Federal OCS and onshore Federal and Indian lands, and distribute those revenues.

Moreover, in working to meet its responsibilities, the **Offshore Minerals Management Program** administers the OCS competitive leasing program and oversees the safe and environmentally sound exploration and production of our Nation's offshore natural gas, oil and other mineral resources. The MMS **Minerals Revenue Management** meets its responsibilities by ensuring the efficient, timely and accurate collection and disbursement of revenue from mineral leasing and production due to Indian tribes and allottees, States and the U.S. Treasury.

The MMS strives to fulfill its responsibilities through the general guiding principles of: (1) being responsive to the public's concerns and interests by maintaining a dialogue with all potentially affected parties and (2) carrying out its programs with an emphasis on working to enhance the quality of life for all Americans by lending MMS assistance and expertise to economic development and environmental protection.

www.ingramcontent.com/pod-product-compliance
Lightning Source LLC
Chambersburg PA
CBHW052001280526
45793CB00005B/814